Justice and Social Policy

A COLLECTION OF ESSAYS

EDITED

WITH AN INTRODUCTION

BY

FREDERICK A. OLAFSON

A SPECTRUM BOOK

PRENTICE-HALL, INC.

Table of Contents

Introduction

Contemporary discussions of the concept of justice have tended to concentrate on the relation of justice to the other virtues—in particular, to the virtue of benevolence. The question they most frequently deal with is whether our duty to be just is logically derivative from our duty to increase the well-being of our fellow human beings. This is in sharp contrast with older views of justice—Plato's for example—which made justice the supreme and all-inclusive social virtue. Such views effectively excluded the possibility that the virtue of justice might, on occasion, bring one into conflict with other demands of social morality. In spite of this difference between ancient and modern approaches to the problem of justice, there is a close connection between them. Indeed, some modern theories of justice are best understood as reactions to certain difficulties implicit in the older accounts, particularly that given by Aristotle. A brief review of the main points of Aristotle's analysis of justice will, therefore, serve as a useful background to the material presented in this volume.

The most distinctive feature of his analysis is its evident assumption that even in the best ordered societies there will be a permanent need for adjudicatory procedures to deal with conflicting claims, and that the rules of justice are, in essence, rules designed to meet this need. Aristotle does not try, as Plato did, to construct a society in which the possibility of conflicts of interest would be eliminated by assigning each person to a strictly delimited sphere of activity to which his natural aptitudes are perfectly suited. Aristotle, it is true, continued to recognize a sense of the term "justice'" in which it stands for complete social virtue; but he was clearly much more interested in a more restricted use of the word. Justice for him means primarily fairness in transactions with others; its opposite is graspingness or a proclivity to take more than one's fair share when some good thing is being distributed. Platonic justice, with its strong affinities to earlier conceptions of justice as cosmic order, has, of course, continued to exert a considerable influence on many minds to this day. But it seems fair to say that Aristotle's shift in emphasis has contributed greatly to the progressive separation of the problem of justice from metaphysical issues and to the recognition that it springs from—and must be resolved within—the social life of human groups. The harmony of individual interests is something to be gradually, though never finally, achieved; it is not a natural condition that must somehow be restored.

Aristotle's second major distinction is between two forms that justice, in his restricted sense, can take. On the one hand, there is distributive justice, which applies in situations in which some good thing—whether it be wealth or honor or something else—is to be divided up among several individuals; on the other, there is rectificatory justice, which corrects distributions that have been improperly made. For each of these, Aristotle presents a formula whose application will insure that all individuals concerned are fairly treated. The central notion that is common to both these formulas is that of proportioning the shares to the merits or deserts of the individuals who receive them. A just distribution is one that is made in such a way that the share any one individual receives stands in the same relation to that of another as the first person does, in point of merit, to the second. In this way, Aristotle tells us, equality in its true sense, which is not that of identical shares for all, is realized. Since Aristotle, like Plato, was convinced that very great differences of natural endowment and moral excellence exist among human beings, it is clear that a just ordering of society, in his view, would have permitted very considerable differences of wealth and privilege.

It must be admitted that from a practical point of view the dependence of Aristotle's rules of justice on the vague concept of desert diminishes their value rather substantially. What, after all, does this desert consist in, and how does one compare the deserts of different persons with one another? To these questions Aristotle gives no answer, and the quasi-mathematical form in which he presents his views does little to alleviate the difficulty. In this connection, it is interesting to note that he is aware of the fact that there are different ways of determining what a man's deserts are. An oligarch, he says, feels that wealth is the chief sign of merit, while the democrat gives greatest weight to free birth. There is no sign, however, that Aristotle regarded the existence of these conflicting criteria as damaging to his general theory of justice. Yet it is just such multiple interpretations of the concept of desert that have counted most heavily against his theory in the long run. Dissatisfaction with this state of affairs came to a head in Jeremy Bentham's decision to clear the boards of moral philosophy by requiring that all the concepts used in appraising and evaluating human actions have a demonstrable relation to the principle of utility. This principle, which Bentham held to be the supreme moral rule, directs us to behave in such a way as to realize the greatest possible amount of happiness for ourselves and others. From this it follows that only those actions that have such an effect are to be regarded as meritorious. But if justice is the distribution of good things in proportion to desert or merit, and the latter is determined by a person's contribution to the sum total of happiness, then justice itself is definable only by reference to the utility-producing tendency of human actions. This in fact seems to have been Bentham's view—at least in so far as the fictitious character which he attributed to justice may be said to have left it any place at all within his system of moral concepts. It is also the view that is defended, although without Bentham's characteristic verve and with a good deal more respect for other points of view, by Henry Sidgwick in the first selection of this book.

Sidgwick's way of arguing his case for the utilitarian theory of justice merits special attention because of its affinities with philosophical procedures that are much in favor at the present time. He begins, not by stating the utilitarian theory of justice, but by trying to reconstruct what he calls the "common notion of justice." By this he means the understanding of justice possessed by ordinary men who are not influenced by philosophical theories of one kind or another—an understanding that is reflected in their characteristic ways of speaking and judging. He then goes on to show that this common notion of justice, while it serves admirably in a wide range of situations, gives rise in others to questions it cannot answer. In general, these are cases in which different claims to just treatment are made on us—claims that conflict and cannot all be satisfied. Here, Sidgwick argues, common sense is at a loss because it has no method for estimating the relative importance of these conflicting claims. At this point in the argument, the utilitarian theory of justice is introduced as an attempt, not to set aside the "common notion of justice," but to deepen and systematize it, thereby enabling it to deal successfully with the questions it cannot answer in its present form. In this capacity utilitarian theory has, of course, its competitors. Sidgwick considers the foremost of these to be intuitionism—the view that when common sense stumbles, recourse may be had to a special and independent intuition of what is right. He concludes, however, that such claims to special insight turn out either to be arbitrary dogmas or to involve a hidden appeal to the principle of utility. Because the latter principle is, in his view, both consistent with the central elements in the common notion of justice and a successful extension of it that permits an otherwise unattainable degree of precision, Sidgwick maintains that it has the strongest claim to acceptance.

Since Sidgwick wrote, the claim that the principle of justice can be derived from the principle of utility has been subjected to close scrutiny. Most of the philosophers who have written on this topic have concluded that the Sidgwick-Bentham thesis is defensible only in some one of a number of modified forms that have been proposed. Others have argued that it has to be abandoned entirely. The three essays that make up the second part of this book have been chosen because in their different ways they are representative of this literature of criticism and revision.

While J. D. Mabbott's essay on "Punishment" deals with only one aspect of the general problem of justice, it has been included not only because it has been widely read and referred to, but also because it is a very concise and clear example of a type of criticism that has often been directed against a certain way of applying the principle of utility—a criticism that can be (and by other writers has been) generalized so as to raise very serious doubts about the traditional mode of formulating the utilitarian social philosophy. Mabbott's central point is that it is unjust to punish a man for any other reason than that he has in fact committed a crime, and that all considerations of the social advantages (deterrence, reform, and so on) produced by such punishment are beside the point. In other words, once there is a rule that makes certain kinds of action crimes, particular punishments are to be justified by reference to that rule and not to the principle of utility. But as Mabbott himself indicates, he is not arguing that considerations of utility are irrelevant to the institution of punishment or to other social institutions; rather, they are properly appealed to only when it is the rules themselves that are under consideration. If he is right, what some writers have called "case-utilitarianism" must give way to "rule-utilitarianism." Moreover, the relation between particular cases, whether of punishment or promise-keeping or whatever, and the principle of utility must be mediated by rules. These rules may have been adopted because they serve the general interest; but once they are adopted, they acquire a kind of functional autonomy.

The essays by Jonathan Harrison and John Rawls both bear on this more sophisticated kind of utilitarianism. Harrison is mainly concerned with the actual task of reformulating utilitarianism in such a way as to make a more adequate place within that doctrine for what he calls our "duty to be just." Rawls, on the other hand, argues that even in its new, two-tiered form utilitarianism cannot yield an adequate theory of justice. He goes on instead to develop in general outline an account of justice as an independent virtue. It may be objected that, since no one of these writers can be called a utilitarian in any but the most qualified sense, the utilitarians are not getting a fair hearing. If a thorough-going defense of an un-repentantly utilitarian theory of justice could have been found, it would certainly have been included. From a survey of the literature, however, it appears that the essays chosen are not just worthy of in-clusion in their own right but are fairly typical of the state of philo-sophical opinion at the present time.

The final section is made up of two essays which originally ap-peared together in a symposium on "Equality." It is clear that while their authors use the terminology of "equality" and "equal rights," what they have in mind is very similar to the fairness and justice of which the other writers in this book speak. On the other hand, these two essays have a distinctive interest, in that they deal with the ques-tion of justice within a broader social and historical frame of refer-ence than do the others. Richard Wollheim's essay is concerned principally with defining the notion of equality that has played so important a role in the Western liberal tradition; Professor Berlin asks what place this ideal of equality should be given among the other ends to which our social policies may be directed. Both essays—Professor Berlin's in particular—may be said to take as their point of departure the assumption (shared, incidentally, by Professor Rawls) that justice is just one of the many virtues that a society may possess. It is a fact that many of the most difficult social questions of our day are at bottom conflicts between the demands of justice and other social goals. There can be little doubt that the virtues of logi-cal acuity and dispassionate analysis, exhibited by the essays in this book, have their own distinctive contribution to make to the solution of those problems.

Part One

Justice

and

Utilitarianism

The Common Notion of Justice: Analysis and Critique

HENRY SIDGWICK

1. We have seen that in delineating the outline of duty, as intuitively recognized, we have to attempt to give to common terms a definite and precise meaning. This process of definition always requires some reflection and care, and is sometimes one of considerable difficulty. But there is no case where the difficulty is greater, or the result more disputed, than when we try to define Justice.

Before making the attempt, it may be as well to remind the reader what it is that we have to do. We have not to enquire into the derivation of the notion of Justice, as we are not now studying the history of our ethical thought, but its actual condition. Nor can we profess to furnish a definition which will correspond to every part of the common usage of the term; for many persons are undoubtedly vague and loose in their application of current moral notions. But it is an assumption of the Intuitional method that the term 'justice' denotes a quality which it is ultimately desirable to realize in the conduct and social relations of men; and that a definition may be given of this which will be accepted by all competent judges as presenting, in a clear and explicit form, what they have always meant by the term, though perhaps implicitly and vaguely. In seeking such a definition we may, so to speak, clip the ragged

From Chapter V of Book III of Sidgwick's *The Methods of Ethics*, 5th edition, 1893.

edge of common usage, but we must not make excision of any considerable portion.

Perhaps the first point that strikes us when we reflect upon our notion of Justice is its connexion with Law. There is no doubt that just conduct is to a great extent determined by Law, and in certain applications the two terms seem interchangeable. Thus we speak indifferently of 'Law Courts' and 'Courts of Justice,' and when a private citizen demands Justice, or his just rights, he commonly means to demand that Law should be carried into effect. Still reflection shows that we do not mean by Justice merely conformity to Law. For, first, we do not always call the violators of law unjust, but only of some Laws: not for example, duellists or gamblers. And secondly, we often judge that Law as it exists does not completely realize Justice; our notion of Justice furnishes a standard with which we compare actual laws, and pronounce them just or unjust. And, thirdly, there is a part of just conduct which lies outside the sphere even of Law as it ought to be; for example, we think that a father may be just or unjust to his children in matters where the law leaves (and ought to leave) him free.

We must then distinguish Justice from what has been called the virtue or duty of Order, or Law-Observance: and perhaps, if we examine the points of divergence just mentioned, we shall be led to the true definition of Justice.

Let us therefore first ask, Of what kind of laws is the observance generally thought to be a realization of Justice? In most cases they might be described as laws which define and secure the interests of assignable individuals. But this description is not complete, as Justice is admittedly concerned in the apportionment of adequate punishment to each offender; though we should not say that a man had an interest in the adequacy of his punishment. Let us say, then, that the laws in which Justice is or ought to be realized, are laws which distribute and allot to individuals either objects of desire, liberties and privileges, or burdens and restraints, or even pains as such. These latter, however, are only allotted by law to persons who have broken other laws. And as all law is enforced by penalties, we see how the administration of law generally may be viewed as the administration of Justice, in accordance with this definition: not because all laws are primarily and in their first intention distributive, but because the execution of law generally involves the due allotment of pains and losses and restraints to the persons who violate it.

Or, more precisely, we should say that this legal distribution *ought* to realize Justice, for we have seen that it may fail to do so. We have next to ask, therefore, What conditions must laws fulfil in order that they may be just in their distributive effects?

Here, however, it may seem that we are transgressing the limit which divides Ethics from Politics: for Ethics is primarily concerned with the rules which ought to govern the private conduct of individuals; and it is commonly thought that private persons ought to obey even laws that they regard as unjust, if established by lawful authority. Still, this is doubted in the case of laws that seem extremely unjust: as (e.g.) the Fugitive Slave law in the United States before the rebellion. At any rate it seems desirable that we should here digress somewhat into political discussion; partly in order to elucidate the notion of Justice, which seems to be essentially the same in both regions, and partly because it is of great practical importance to individuals, in regulating private conduct beyond the range of Law-observance, to know whether the laws and established order of the society in which they live are just or unjust.

Now perhaps the most obvious and commonly recognized characteristic of just laws is that they are Equal: and in some departments of legislation, at least, the common notion of Justice seems to be exhaustively expressed by that of Equality. It is commonly thought, for example, that a system of taxation would be perfectly just if it imposed exactly equal burdens upon all: and though this notion of 'equal burden' is itself somewhat difficult to define with the precision required for practical application, still we may say that Justice here is thought to resolve itself into a kind of equality. However, we cannot affirm generally that all laws ought to affect all persons equally, for this would leave no place for any laws allotting special privileges and burdens to special classes of the community; but we do not think all such laws necessarily unjust: e.g. we think it not unjust that only persons appointed in a certain way should share in legislation, and that men should be forced to fight for their country but not women. Hence some have said that the only sense in which Justice requires a law to be equal is that its execution must affect equally all the individuals belonging to any of the classes specified in the law. And no doubt this rule excludes a very real kind of injustice: it is of the highest importance that judges and administrators should never be persuaded by money or otherwise to show 'respect of persons.'

So much equality, however, is involved in the very notion of a law, if it be couched in general terms: and it is plain that laws may be equally executed and yet unjust: for example, we should consider a law unjust which compelled only red-haired men to serve in the army, even though it were applied with the strictest impartiality to all red-haired men. We must therefore conclude, that, in laying down the law no less than in carrying it out, all inequality affecting the interests of individuals which appears arbitrary, and for which no sufficient reason can be given, is held to be unjust. But we have still to ask, what kind of reasons for inequality Justice admits and from what general principle (or principles) all such reasons are to be deduced?

2. Perhaps we shall find it easier to answer this question, if we examine the notion of Justice as applied to that part of private conduct which lies beyond the sphere of law. Here, again, we may observe that the notion of Justice always involves allotment of something considered as advantageous or disadvantageous: whether it be money or other material means of happiness; or praise, or affection, or other immaterial good, or some merited pain or loss. Hence I should answer the question raised in the preceding chapter as to the classification of the duties there discussed under the heads of Justice and Benevolence respectively, by saying that the fulfilment of any duty of the affections, considered by itself, does not exemplify Justice: but that when we come to compare the obligations arising out of different affectionate relations, and to consider the right allotment of love and kind services, the notion of Justice becomes applicable. In order to arrange this allotment properly we have to inquire what is Just. What then do we mean by a just man in matters where law-observance does not enter? It is natural to reply that we mean an impartial man, one who seeks with equal care to satisfy all claims which he recognizes as valid and does not let himself be unduly influenced by personal preferences. And this seems an adequate account of the virtue of justice so far as we consider it merely subjectively, and independently of the intellectual insight required for the realization of objective justice in action: if we neglect to give due consideration to any claim which we regard as reasonable, our action cannot be just in intention. This definition suffices to exclude wilful injustice: but it is obvious that it does not give us a sufficient criterion of just acts, any more than the absence of arbitrary inequality was found to be a suffi-

cient criterion of just laws. We want to know what are reasonable claims.

Well, of these the most important—apart from the claims discussed in the preceding chapter—seems to be that resulting from contract. This is to a certain extent enforced by law: but it is clear to us that a just man will keep engagements generally, even when there may be no legal penalty attached to their violation. The exact definition of this duty, and its commonly submitted qualifications, will be discussed in the next chapter: but of its general bindingness Common Sense has no doubt.

Further, we include under the idea of binding engagements not merely verbal promises, but also what are called 'implied contracts,' or 'tacit understandings.' But this latter term is a difficult one to keep precise: and, in fact, is often used to include not only the case where A has in some way positively implied a pledge to B, but also the case where B has certain expectations of which A is aware. Here, however, the obligation is not so clear: for it would hardly be said that a man is bound to dispel all erroneous expectations that he may know to be formed respecting his conduct, at the risk of being required to fulfill them. Still, if the expectation was such as most persons would form under the circumstances, there seems to be some sort of moral obligation to fulfil it, if it does not conflict with other duties, though the obligation seems less definite and stringent than that arising out of contract. Indeed I think we may say that Justice is generally, though somewhat vaguely, held to prescribe the fulfilment of all such expectations (of services, etc.) as arise naturally and normally out of the relations, voluntary or involuntary, in which we stand towards other human beings. But the discussions in the preceding chapter have shown the difficulty of defining even those duties of this kind which, in an indefinite form, seemed certain and indisputable: while others are only defined by customs which to reflection appear arbitrary. And though while these customs persist, the expectations springing from them are in a certain sense natural, so that a just man seems to be under a kind of obligation to fulfil them, this obligation cannot be regarded as clear or complete, for two reasons that were given in the last chapter; first, because customs are continually varying, and as long as any one is in a state of variation, growing or decaying, the validity of the customary claim is obviously doubtful; and secondly, because it does not seem right that an irrational and inexpedient custom should last for ever, and yet it can only be abolished by being "more honoured in the breach than in the observance."

This line of reflection therefore has landed us in a real perplexity respecting the department of duty which we are at present examining. Justice is something that we conceive to be intrinsically capable of perfectly definite determination: a scrupulously just man, we think, must be very exact and precise in his conduct. But when we consider that part of Justice which consists in satisfying such natural and customary claims as arise independently of contract, it seems impossible to estimate these claims with any exactness. The attempt to map out the region of Justice reveals to us a sort of margin or dim borderland, tenanted by expectations which are not quite claims and with regard to which we do not feel sure whether Justice does or does not require us to satisfy them. For the ordinary actions of men proceed on the expectation that the future will resemble the past; hence it seems natural to expect that any particular man will do as others do in similar circumstances, and, still more, that he will continue to do whatever he has hitherto been in the habit of doing; accordingly his fellow-men are inclined to think themselves wronged by his suddenly omitting any customary or habitual act, if the omission causes them loss or inconvenience. On the other hand, if a man has given no pledge to maintain a custom or habit, it seems hard that he should be bound by the unwarranted expectations of others. In this perplexity, common sense often appears to decide differently cases similar in all respects, except in the quantity of disappointment caused by the change. For instance, if a poor man were to leave one tradesman and deal with another because the first had turned Quaker, we should hardly call it an act of injustice, however unreasonable we might think it: but if a rich country gentleman were to act similarly towards a poor neighbour, many persons would say that it was unjust persecution.

The difficulty just pointed out extends equally to the duties of kindness—even to the specially stringent and sacred duties of the domestic affections and gratitude—discussed in the previous chapter. We cannot get any new principle for settling any conflict that may present itself among such duties, by asking 'what Justice requires of us': the application of the notion of Justice only leads us to view the problem in a new aspect—as a question of the right *distribution* of kind services—it does not help us to solve it. Had we clear and precise intuitive principles for determining the claims (e.g.) of parents on children, children on parents, benefactors on the recipients of their benefits, we might say exactly at what point or to what extent the satisfaction of one of these claims ought in justice to be postponed to the satisfaction of another, or to any worthy aim of a different kind: but I know no method of determining a problem of this kind which is not either implicitly utilitarian, or arbitrarily dogmatic, and unsupported by Common Sense.

3. If now we turn again to the political question, from which we diverged, we see that we have obtained from the preceding discussion one of the criteria of the justice of laws which we were seeking—*viz.* that they must avoid running counter to natural and normal expectations—: but we see at the same time that the criterion cannot be made definite in its application to private conduct, and it is easy to show that there is the same indefiniteness and consequent difficulty in applying it to legislation. For Law itself is a main source of natural expectations; and, since in ordinary times the alterations in law are very small in proportion to the amount unaltered, there is always a natural expectation that the existing laws will be maintained: and although this is, of course, an indefinite and uncertain expectation in a society like ours, where laws are continually being altered by lawful authority, it is sufficient for people in general to rely upon in arranging their concerns, investing their money, choosing their place of abode, their trade and profession, etc. Hence, when such expectations are disappointed by a change in the law, the disappointed persons complain of injustice, and it is to some extent admitted that justice requires that they should be compensated for the loss thus incurred. But such expectations are of all degrees of definiteness and importance, and generally extend more widely as they decrease in value, like the ripples made by throwing a stone into a pond, so that it is practically impossible to compensate them all: at the same time, I know no intuitive principle by which we could separate valid claims from invalid, and distinguish injustice from simple hardship.

But even if this difficulty were overcome further reflection must, I think, show that the criterion above given is incomplete or imperfectly stated: otherwise it would appear that no old law could be unjust, since laws that have existed for a long time must create corresponding expectations. But this is contrary to Common Sense: as we are continually becoming convinced that old laws are unjust (e.g. laws establishing slavery): indeed, this continually recurring conviction seems to be one of the great sources of change in the laws of a progressive society.

Perhaps we may say that there are natural expectations which grow up from other elements of the social order, independent of and so possibly conflicting with laws: and that we call rules unjust which go counter to these. Thus e.g. primogeniture appears to many unjust, because all the landowner's children are brought up in equally luxurious habits, and share equally the paternal care and expenditure, and so the inequality of inheritance seems paradoxical and harsh. Still, we cannot explain every case in this way: for example, the conviction that slavery is unjust can hardly be traced to anything in the established order of the slaveholding society, but seems to arise in a different way.

The truth is, this notion of 'natural expectations' is worse than indefinite: the ambiguity of the term conceals a fundamental conflict of ideas, which appears more profound and far-reaching in its consequences the more we examine it. For the word 'natural,' as used in this connexion, covers and conceals the whole chasm between the actual and the ideal —what is and what ought to be. As we before noticed, the term seems, as ordinarily used, to contain the distinct ideas of (1) the common as opposed to the exceptional, and (2) the original or primitive as contrasted with the result of later conventions and institutions. But it is also used to signify, in more or less indefinite combination with one or other of these meanings, 'what would exist in an ideal state of society.' And it is easy to see how these different meanings have been blended and confounded. For since by 'Nature' men have really meant God, or God viewed in a particular aspect—God, we may say, as known to us in experience—when they have come to conceive a better state of things than that which actually exists, they have not only regarded this ideal state as really exhibiting the Divine purposes more than the actual, and as being so far more 'natural': but they have gone further, and supposed more or less definitely that this ideal state of things must be what God originally created, and that the defects recognizable in what now exists must be due to the deteriorating action of men. But if we dismiss this latter view, as unsupported by historical evidence, we recognize more plainly the contrast and conflict between the other two meanings of 'natural,' and the corresponding discrepancy between the two elements of the common notion of Justice. For, from one point of view, we are disposed to think that the *customary* distribution of rights, goods, and privileges, as well as burdens and pains, is natural and just, and that this ought to be maintained by law, as it usually is: while, from another point of view, we seem to recognize an ideal system of rules of distribution which ought to exist, but perhaps have never yet existed, and we consider laws to be just in proportion as they conform to this ideal. It is the reconciliation between these two views which is the chief problem of political Justice.[1]

On what principles, then, is the ideal to be determined? This is, in fact, the question which has been chiefly in view from the outset of the chapter; but we could not satisfactorily discuss it until we had distinguished the two elements of Justice, as commonly conceived—one conservative of law and custom, and the other tending to reform them. It is on this latter that we shall now concentrate our attention.

When, however, we examine this Ideal, as it seems to show itself in the minds of different men in different ages and countries, we observe various forms of it, which it is important to distinguish.

In the first place, it must be noticed that an ideal constitution of society may be conceived and sought with many other ends in view besides the right distribution of good and evil among the individuals that compose it: as (e.g.) with a view to conquest and success in war, or to the development of industry and commerce, or to the highest possible cultivation of the arts and sciences. But any such political ideal as this is beyond the range of our present consideration, as it is not constructed on the basis of our common notion of Justice. Our present question is, Are there any clear principles from which we may work out an ideally just distribution of rights and privileges, burdens and pains, among human beings as such? There is a widespread view, that in order to make society just certain Natural Rights should be conceded to all members of the community, and that positive law should at least embody and protect these, whatever other regulations it may contain: but it is difficult to find in Common Sense any definite agreement in the enumeration of these Natural Rights, still less any clear principles from which they can be systematically deduced.

---

[1] It is characteristic of an unprogressive society that in it these two points of view are indistinguishable; the Jural Ideal absolutely coincides with the Customary, and social perfection is imagined to consist in the perfect observance of a traditional system of rules.

4. There is, however, one mode of systematizing these Rights and bringing them under one principle, which has been maintained by influential thinkers; and which, though now perhaps somewhat antiquated, is still sufficiently current to deserve careful examination. It has been held that Freedom from interference is really the whole of what human beings, originally and apart from contracts, can be strictly said to *owe* to each other: at any rate, that the protection of this Freedom (including the enforcement of Free Contract) is the sole proper aim of Law i.e. of those rules of mutual behaviour which are maintained by penalties inflicted under the authority of Government. All natural Rights, on this view, may be summed up in the Right to Freedom; so that the complete attainment of this would be the complete realization of Justice,—the Equality at which Justice is thought to aim being interpreted in this special sense of Equality of Freedom.

Now when I contemplate this as an abstract formula, though I cannot say that it is self-evident to me as the true fundamental principle of Ideal Law, I admit that it commends itself much to my mind; and I might perhaps persuade myself that it is owing to the defect of my faculty of moral (or jural) intuition that I fail to see its self-evidence. But when I endeavour to bring it into closer relation to the actual circumstances of human society, it soon comes to wear a different aspect.

In the first place, it seems obviously needful to limit the extent of its application. For it involves the negative principle that no one should be coerced for his own good alone; but no one would gravely argue that this ought to be applied to the case of children, or of idiots, or insane persons. But if so, can we know *a priori* that it ought to be applied to all sane adults? since the above-mentioned exceptions are commonly justified on the ground that children, etc. will manifestly be better off if they are forced to do and abstain as others think best for them; and it is, at least, not intuitively certain that the same argument does not apply to the majority of mankind in the present state of their intellectual progress. Indeed, it is often conceded by the advocates of this principle that it does not hold even in respect of adults in a low state of civilization. But if so, what criterion can be given for its application, except that it must be applied wherever human beings are sufficiently intelligent to provide for themselves better than others would provide for them? and thus the principle would present itself not as absolute and recognized by an independent intuition, but as a subordinate application of the principle of aiming at the general good.

But again, the term Freedom is ambiguous. If we interpret it strictly, as meaning Freedom of Action alone, the principle seems to allow any amount of mutual annoyance except constraint. But obviously no one would be satisfied with such Freedom as this. If, however, we include in the idea absence of pain and annoyance inflicted by others, it becomes at once evident that we cannot prohibit all such annoyances without restraining freedom of action to a degree that would be intolerable; since there is scarcely any gratification of a man's natural impulses which may not cause some annoyance to others. Hence in distinguishing the mutual annoyances that ought to be allowed from those that must be prohibited we seem forced to balance the evils of constraint against pain and loss of a different kind: while if we admit the Utilitarian criterion so far, it is difficult to maintain that annoyance to individuals is never to be permitted in order to attain any positive good result, but only to prevent more serious annoyance.

Thirdly, in order to render a social construction possible on this basis, we must assume that the right to Freedom includes the right to limit one's freedom by contract; and that such contracts, if they are really voluntary and not obtained by fraud or force, and if they do not violate the freedom of others, are to be enforced by legal penalties. But, in the first place, it does not seem clear that enforcement of Contracts is strictly included in the notion of realizing Freedom; for a man seems to be most completely free when no one of his volitions is allowed to have any effect in causing the *external* coercion of any other. And, again, it may be asked whether this right of limiting Freedom is itself unlimited, and whether a man may thus freely contract himself out of freedom into slavery. For in this case the principle of freedom seems in a manner suicidal; and yet it is hard to see how from this principle any limitation of the right of contract can be deduced.

But if it be difficult to define Freedom as an ideal to be realized in the merely personal relations of human beings, the difficulty is increased when we consider the relation of men to the material means of life and happiness.

For it is commonly thought that the individual's right to Freedom includes the right of appropriating material things. But if Freedom be understood strictly, I do not see that it implies more than his right to non-interference while actually using such things as can only be used by one person at once: the right to prevent others from using at any future time anything that an individual has once seized seems an interference with the free action of others beyond what is needed to secure the freedom, strictly speaking, of the appropriator. It may perhaps be said that a man, in appropriating a particular thing, does not interfere with the freedom of others, because the rest of the world is still open to them. But others may want just what he has appropriated: and they may not be able to find anything so good at all, or at least without much labour and search; for many of the instruments and materials of comfortable living are limited in quantity. This argument applies especially to property in land: and it is to be observed that, in this case, there is a further difficulty in determining how much a man is to be allowed to appropriate by 'first occupation.' If it be said that a man is to be understood to occupy what he is able to use, the answer is obvious that the use of land by any individual may vary almost indefinitely in extent, while diminishing proportionally in intensity. For instance, it would surely be a paradoxcal deduction from the principle of Freedom to maintain that an individual had a right to exclude others from pasturing sheep on any part of the land over which his hunting expeditions could extend. But if so can it be clear that a shepherd has such a right against one who wishes to till the land, or that one who is using the surface has a right to exclude a would-be miner? I do not see how the deduction is to be made out. Again, it may be disputed whether the right of Property, as thus derived, is to include the right of controlling the disposal of one's possessions after death. For this to most persons seems naturally bound up with ownership: yet it is paradoxical to say that we interfere with a man's freedom of action by anything that we may do after his death to what he owned during his life: and jurists have often treated this right as purely conventional and not therefore included in 'natural law.'

Other difficulties might be raised: but we need not pursue them, for if Freedom be taken simply to mean that one man's actions are to be as little as possible restrained by others, it is obviously more fully realized without appropriation. And if it be said that it includes, besides this, facility and security in the gratification of desires, and that it is Freedom in this sense that we think should be equally distributed, and that this cannot be realized without appropriation; then it may be replied, that in a society where nearly all material things are already appropriated, this kind of Freedom is not and cannot be equally distributed. A man born into such a society, without inheritance, is not only far less free than those who possess property, but he is less free than if there had been no appropriation. It may be said that, having freedom of contract, he will give his services in exchange for the means of satisfying his wants; and that this exchange must necessarily give him more than he could have got if he had been placed in the world by himself; that, in fact, any human society always renders the part of the earth that it inhabits more capable of affording gratification of desires to each and all of its later-born members than it would otherwise be. But however true this may be as a general rule, it is obviously not so in all cases: as men are sometimes unable to sell their services at all, and often can only obtain in exchange for them an insufficient subsistence. And, even granting it to be true, it does not prove that society, by appropriation, has not interfered with the natural freedom of its poorer members: but only that it compensates them for such interference, and that the compensation is adequate: and it must be evident that if compensation in the form of material commodities can be justly given for an encroachment on Freedom, the realization of Freedom cannot be the one ultimate end of distributive Justice.

5. It seems, then, that though Freedom is an object of keen and general desire, and an important source of happiness, both in itself and indirectly from the satisfaction of natural impulses which it allows, the attempt to make it the fundamental notion of theoretical Jurisprudence is attended with insuperable difficulties: and that even the Natural Rights which it claims to cover cannot be brought under it except in a very forced and arbitrary manner. But further, even if this were otherwise, an equal distribution of Freedom does not seem to exhaust our notion of Justice. Ideal Justice, as we commonly conceive it, seems to demand that not only Freedom but all other benefits and burdens should be distributed, if not equally, at any rate justly,—Justice in distribution being regarded as not identical with Equality, but merely exclusive of arbitrary inequality.

How, then, shall we find the principle of this highest and most comprehensive ideal?

We shall be led to it, I think, by referring again to one of the grounds of obligation to render services, which was noticed in the last chapter: the claim of Gratitude. It there appeared that we have not only a natural impulse to requite benefits, but also a conviction that such requital is a duty, and its omission blameworthy, to some extent at least; though we find it difficult to define the extent. Now it seems that when we, so to say, *universalize* this impulse and conviction, we get the element in the common view of Justice, which we are now trying to define. For if we take the proposition 'that good done to any individual ought to be requited by him,' and leave out the relation to the individual in either term of the proposition, we seem to have an equally strong conviction of the truth of the more general statement 'that good deeds ought to be requited.' And if we take into consideration all the different kinds and degrees of services, upon the mutual exchange of which society is based, we get the proposition 'that men ought to be rewarded in proportion to their deserts.' And this would be commonly held to be the true and simple principle of distribution in any case where there are no claims arising from Contract or Custom to modify its operation.

For example, it would be admitted that—if there has been no previous arrangement—the profits of any work or enterprise should be divided among those who have contributed to its success in proportion to the worth of their services. And it may be observed, that some thinkers maintain the proposition discussed in the previous section—that Law ought to aim at securing the greatest possible Freedom for each in-dividual—not as absolute and axiomatic, but as derivative from the principle that Desert ought to be requited; on the ground that the best way of providing for the requital of Desert is to leave men as free as possible to exert themselves for the satisfaction of their own desires, and so to win each his own requital. And this seems to be really the principle upon which the Right of Property is rested, when it is justi-fied by the proposition that 'every one has an exclusive right to the produce of his labour.' For on reflection it is seen that no labour really 'produces' any material thing, but only adds to its value: and we do not think that a man can acquire a right to a material thing belonging to another, by spending his labour on it—even if he does so in the *bona fide* belief that it is his own property—but only to adequate *com-pensation* for his labour; this, therefore, is what the proposition just quoted must mean. The principle is, indeed, sometimes stretched to explain the original right of property in materials, as being in a sense 'produced' (i.e., found) by their first discoverer;[2] but here again, reflection shows that Common Sense does not grant this (as a *moral* right) absolutely, but only in so far as it appears to be not more than adequate compensation for the discoverer's trouble. For example, we should not consider that the first finder of a large uninhabited region had a moral right to appropriate the whole of it. Hence this justification of the right of property refers us ultimately to the principle 'that every man ought to receive adequate requital for his labour.' So, again, when we speak of the world as justly governed by God, we seem to mean that, if we could know the whole of human existence, we should find that happiness is distributed among men according to their deserts. And Divine Justice is thought to be a pattern which Human Justice is to imitate as far as the conditions of human society allow.

This kind of Justice, as has been said, seems like Gratitude universalized: and the same principle applied to punishment may similarly be regarded as Resentment universalized; though the parallel is incomplete, if we are considering the present state of our moral conceptions. History shows us a time in which it was thought not only as natural, but as clearly right and incumbent on a man, to requite injuries as to repay benefits: but as moral reflection developed in Europe this notion was repudiated, so that Plato taught that it could never be right really to harm any one, however he may have harmed us. And this is the accepted doctrine in Christian societies, as regards requital by individuals of personal wrongs. But in its universalized form the old conviction still lingers in the popular view of Criminal Justice: it seems still to be widely held that Justice requires pain to be inflicted on a man who has done wrong, even if no benefit result either to him or to others from the pain. Personally, I am so far from holding this view that I have an instinctive and strong moral aversion to it: and I hesitate to attribute it to Common Sense, since I think that it is gradually passing

---

[2] It certainly requires a considerable strain to bring the 'right of First Discovery' under the notion of 'right to the produce of one's labour.' Hence Locke and others have found it necessary to suppose, as the ultimate justification of the former right, 'a tacit consent' of mankind in general that all things previously unappropriated shall belong to the first appropriator. But this must be admitted to be a rather desperate device of ethico-political construction: on account of the fatal facility with which it may be used to justify almost any arbitrariness in positive law.

away from the moral consciousness of educated persons in the most advanced communities: but I think it is still perhaps the more ordinary view.

This, then, is one element of what Aristotle calls Corrective Justice, which is embodied in criminal law. It must not be confounded with the principle of Reparation, on which legal awards of damages are based. We have already noticed this as a simple deduction from the maxim of general Benevolence, which forbids us to do harm to our fellow-creatures: for if we have harmed them, we can yet approximately obey the maxim by giving compensation for the harm. Though here the question arises whether we are bound to make reparation for harm that has been quite blamelessly caused: and it is not easy to answer it decisively. On the whole, I think we should condemn a man who did not offer some reparation for any serious injury caused by him to another—even if quite involuntarily caused, and without negligence: but perhaps we regard this rather as a duty of Benevolence—arising out of the general sympathy that each ought to have for others, intensified by this special occasion—than as a duty of strict Justice. If, however, we limit the requirement of Reparation, under the head of strict Justice, to cases in which the mischief repaired is due to acts or omissions in some degree culpable, a difficulty arises from the divergence between the moral view of culpability, and that which social security requires. Of this I will speak presently. In any case there is now no danger of confusion or collision between the principle of Reparative and that of Retributive Justice, as the one is manifestly concerned with the claims of the injured party, and the other with the deserts of the wrong-doer: though in the actual administration of Law the obligation of paying compensation for wrong may sometimes be treated as a sufficient punishment for the wrongdoer.

When however we turn again to the other branch of Retributive Justice, which is concerned with the reward of services, we find another notion, which I will call Fitness, often blended indistinguishably with the notion of Desert, and so needing to be carefully separated from it; and when the distinction has been made, we see that the two are liable to come into collision. I do not feel sure that the principle of 'distribution according to Fitness' is found, strictly speaking, in the analysis of the ordinary notion of Justice: but it certainly enters into our common conception of the ideal or perfectly rational order of society, as regards the distribution both of instruments and functions, and (to some extent at least) of other sources of happiness. We certainly think it reasonable that instruments should be given to those who can use them best, and functions allotted to those who are most competent to perform them: but these may not be those who have rendered most services in the past. And again, we think it reasonable that particular material means of enjoyment should fall to the lot of those who are susceptible of the respective kinds of pleasure; as no one would think of allotting pictures to a blind man, or rare wines to one who had no taste: hence we should probably think it fitting that artists should have larger shares than mechanics in the social distribution of wealth, though they may be by no means more deserving. Thus the notions of Desert and Fitness appear at least occasionally conflicting: but perhaps, as I have suggested, Fitness should rather be regarded as a utilitarian principle of distribution, inevitably limiting the realization of what is abstractly just, than as a part of the interpretation of Justice proper: and it is with the latter that we are at present concerned. At any rate it is the Requital of Desert that constitutes the chief element of Ideal Justice, in so far as this imports something more than mere Equality and Impartiality. Let us then examine more closely wherein Desert consists; and we will begin with Good Desert or Merit, as being of the most fundamental and permanent importance; for we may hope that crime and its punishment will decrease and gradually disappear as the world improves, but the right or best distribution of the means of wellbeing is an object that we must always be striving to realize.

6. And first, the question which we had to consider in defining Gratitude again recurs: whether, namely, we are to apportion the reward to the effort made, or to the results attained. For it may be said that the actual utility of any service must depend much upon favourable circumstances and fortunate accidents, not due to any desert of the agent: or again, may be due to powers and skills which were connate, or have been developed by favourable conditions of life, or by good education, and why should we reward him for these? (for the last-mentioned we ought rather to reward those who have educated him). And certainly it is only in so far as *moral* excellences are exhibited in human achievements that they are commonly thought to be such as God will reward. But by drawing this line we do not yet get rid of the difficulty. For it

may still be said that good actions are due entirely, or to a great extent, to good dispositions and habits, and that these are partly inherited and partly due to the care of parents and teachers; so that in rewarding these we are rewarding the results of natural and accidental advantages, and it is unreasonable to distinguish these from others, such as skill and knowledge, and to say that it is even ideally just to reward the one and not the other. Shall we say, then, that the reward should be proportionate to the amount of voluntary effort for a good end? But Determinists will say that even this is ultimately the effect of causes extraneous to the man's self. On the Determinist view, then, it would seem to be ideally just (if anything is so) that all men should enjoy equal amounts of happiness: for there seems to be no justice in making A happier than B, merely because circumstances beyond his own control have first made him better. But why should we not, instead of 'all men,' say 'all sentient beings'? for why should man have more happiness than any other animal? But thus the pursuit of ideal justice seems to conduct us to such a precipice of paradox that Common Sense is likely to abandon it. At any rate the ordinary idea of Desert has thus altogether vanished.[3] And thus we seem to be led to the conclusion which I anticipated in Bk. I. ch. V.: that in this one department of our moral consciousness the idea of Free Will seems involved in a peculiar way in the moral ideas of Common Sense, since if it is eliminated the important notions of Desert or Merit and Justice require material modification.[4] At the same time, the difference between Determinist and Libertarian Justice can hardly have any practical effect. For in any case it does not seem possible

[3] The only tenable Determinist interpretation of Desert is, in my opinion, the Utilitarian: according to which, when a man is said to deserve reward for any services to society, the meaning is that it is expedient to reward him, in order that he and others may be induced to render similar services by the expectation of similar rewards. Cf. *post*, Book IV ch. iii §4.

[4] Perhaps we may partly attribute to the difficulties above discussed, that the notion of Desert has sometimes dropped out of the ideal of Utopian reconstructors of society, and 'Equality of Happiness' has seemed to be the only end. Justice, it has been thought, prescribes simply that each should have an equal share of happiness, as far as happiness depends on the action of others. But there seems to be much difficulty in working this out: for (apart from the considerations of Fitness above mentioned) equal happiness is not to be attained by equal distribution of objects of desire. For some require more and some less to be equally happy. Hence, it seems, we must take differences of *needs* into consideration. But if merely mental needs are included (as seems reasonable) we should have to give less to cheerful, contented, self-sacrificing people than to those who are naturally moody and *exigeant,* as the former can be made happy with less. And this is too paradoxical to recommend itself to Common Sense.

to separate in practice that part of a man's achievement which is due strictly to his free choice from that part which is due to the original gift of nature and to favouring circumstances:[5] so that we must necessarily leave to Providence the realization of what we conceive as the theoretical ideal of Justice, and content ourselves with trying to reward voluntary actions in proportion to the worth of the services intentionally rendered by them.

If, then, we take as the principle of ideal justice, so far as this can be practically aimed at in human society, the requital of voluntary services in proportion to their worth, it remains to consider on what principle or principles the comparative worth of different services is to be rationally estimated. There is no doubt that we commonly assume such an estimate to be possible; for we continually speak of the 'fair' or 'proper' price of any kind of services as something generally known, and condemn the demand for more than this as extortionate. It may be said that the notion of Fairness or Equity which we ordinarily apply in such judgments is to be distinguished from that of Justice; Equity being in fact often contrasted with strict Justice, and conceived as capable of coming into collision with it. And this is partly true: but I think the wider and no less usual sense of the term Justice, in which it includes Equity or Fairness, is the only one that can be conveniently adopted in an ethical treatise: for in any case where Equity comes into conflict with strict justice, its dictates are held to be in a higher sense just, and what ought to be ultimately carried into effect in the case considered—though, not, perhaps, by the administrators of law. I treat Equity, therefore, as a species of Justice; though noting that the former term is more ordinarily used in cases where the definiteness attainable is recognized as somewhat less than in ordinary cases of rightful claims arising out of law or contract. On what principle, then, can we determine the 'fair' or 'equitable' price of services? When we examine the common judgments of practical persons in which this judgment occurs, we find, I think, that

[5] No doubt, it would be possible to remove, to some extent, the inequalities that are attributable to circumstances, by bringing the best education within the reach of all classes, so that all children might have an equal opportunity of being selected and trained for any functions for which they seemed to be fit: and this seems to be prescribed by ideal justice, in so far as it removes or mitigates arbitrary inequality. Accordingly in those ideal reconstructions of society, in which we may expect to find men's notions of abstract justice exhibited, such an institution as this has generally found a place. Still, there will be much natural inequality which we cannot remove or even estimate.

the 'fair' in such cases is ascertained by a reference to analogy and custom, and that any service is considered to be 'fairly worth' what is usually given for services of the kind. Hence this element of the notion of Justice may seem, after all, to resolve itself into that discussed in §2: and in some states of society it certainly appears that the payment to be given for services is as completely fixed by usage as any other customary duty, so that it would be a clear disappointment of normal expectation to deviate from this usage. But probably no one in a modern civilised community would maintain in its full breadth this identification of the Just with the Usual price of services: and so far as the judgments of practical persons may seem to imply this, I think it must be admitted that they are superficial or merely inadvertent, and ignore the established mode of determining the market prices of commodities by free competition of producers and traders. For where such competition operates the market value rises and falls, and is different at different places and times; so that no properly instructed person can expect any fixity in it, or complain of injustice merely on account of the variations in it.

Can we then say that 'market value' (as determined by free competition) corresponds to our notion of what is ideally just?

This is a question of much interest, because this is obviously the mode of determining the remuneration of services that would be universal in a society constructed on the principle previously discussed, of securing the greatest possible Freedom to all members of the community. It should be observed that this, which we may call the Individualistic Ideal, is the type to which modern civilised communities have, until lately, been tending to approximate: and it is therefore very important to know whether it is one which completely satisfies the demands of morality; and whether Freedom, if not an absolute end or First Principle of abstract Justice, is still to be sought as the best means to the realization of a just social order by the general requital of Desert.

At first sight it seems plausible to urge that the 'market value' represents the estimate set upon anything by mankind generally, and therefore gives us exactly that 'common sense' judgment respecting value which we are now trying to find. But on examination it seems likely that the majority of men are not properly qualified to decide on the value of many important kinds of services, from imperfect knowledge of their nature and effects; so that, as far as these are concerned, the true judgment will not be represented in the market place. Even in the case of things which a man is generally able to estimate, it may be manifest in a particular case that he is ignorant of the real utility of what he exchanges; and in this case the 'free' contract hardly seems to be fair: though if the ignorance was not caused by the other party to the exchange, Common Sense is hardly prepared to condemn the latter as unjust for taking advantage of it. For instance, if a man has discovered by a legitimate use of geological knowledge and skill that there is probably a valuable mine on land owned by a stranger, reasonable persons would not blame him for concealing his discovery until he had bought the mine at its market value: yet it could not be said that the seller got what it was really worth. In fact Common Sense is rather perplexed on this point: and the *rationale* of the conclusion at which it arrives, must, I conceive, be sought in economic considerations, which take us quite beyond the analysis of the common notion of Justice.

Again, there are social services recognized as highly important which generally speaking have no price in any market, on account of the indirectness and uncertainty of their practical utility: as, for instance, scientific discoveries. The extent to which any given discovery will aid industrial invention is so uncertain, that even if the secret of it could be conveniently kept, it would not usually be profitable to buy it.

But even if we confine our attention to products and services generally marketable, and to bargains thoroughly understood on both sides, there are still serious difficulties in the way of identifying the notions of 'free' and 'fair' exchange. Thus, where an individual, or combination of individuals, has the monopoly of a certain kind of services, the market-price of the aggregate of such services can under certain conditions be increased by diminishing their total amount; but it would seem absurd to say that the social Desert of those rendering the services is thereby increased, and a plain man has grave doubts whether the price thus attained is fair. Still less is it thought fair to take advantage of the transient monopoly produced by emergency: thus, if I saw Croesus drowning and no one near, it would not be held fair in me to refuse to save him except at the price of half his wealth. But if so, can it be fair for any class of persons to gain competitively by the unfavourable economic situation of another class with which they deal? And if we admit that it would be unfair, where are we to draw the line? For any increase of the numbers of a class renders its situation for bargaining less favourable: since the market price of different services depends partly upon the ease or difficulty of procuring them—as Political Economists say, 'on the relation between the supply of services and the demand for them'—and it does not seem that any individual's social Desert can properly be lessened merely by the increased number or willingness of others rendering the same services. Nor, indeed, does it seem that it can be decreased by his own willingness, for it is strange to reward a man less because he is zealous and eager in the performance of his function; yet in bargaining the less willing always has the advantage. And, finally, it hardly appears that the social worth of a man's service is necessarily increased by the fact that his service is rendered to those who can pay lavishly; but his reward is certainly likely to be greater from this cause.

Such considerations as these have led some political thinkers to hold that Justice requires a mode of distributing payment for services, entirely different from that at present effected by free competition: and that all labourers ought to be paid according to the intrinsic value of their labour as estimated by enlightened and competent judges. If this Socialistic Ideal—as we may perhaps call it—could be realized without counter-balancing evils, it would certainly seem to give a nearer approximation to what we conceive as Divine Justice than the present state of society affords. But this supposes that we have found the rational method of determining value: which, however, is still to seek. Shall we say that these judges are to take the value of a service as proportionate to the amount of happiness produced by it? If so, the calculation is, of course, exposed to all the difficulties of the hedonistic method discussed in Book II.: but supposing these can be overcome, it is still hard to say how we are to compare the value of different services that must necessarily be combined to produce happy life. For example, how shall we compare the respective values of necessaries and luxuries? for we may be more sensible of the enjoyment derived from the latter, but we could not have this at all without the former. And again, when different kinds of labour cooperate in the same production, how are we to estimate their relative values? for even if all mere unskilled labour may be brought to a common standard, this seems almost impossible in the case of different kinds of skill. For how shall we compare the labour of design with that of achievement? or the supervision of the whole with the execution of details? or the labour of actually producing with that of educating producers? or the service of the *savant* who discovers a new principle, with that of the inventor who applies it?

I do not see how these questions, or the difficulties noticed in the preceding paragraph, can be met by any analysis of our common notion of Justice. To deal with such points at all satisfactorily we have, I conceive, to adopt quite a different line of reasoning: we have to ask, not what services of a certain kind are intrinsically worth, but what reward can procure them and whether the rest of society gain by the services more than the equivalent reward. We have, in short, to give up as impracticable the construction of an ideally just social order, in which all services are rewarded in exact proportion to their intrinsic value. And, for similar reasons, we seem forced to conclude, more generally, that it is impossible to obtain clear premises for a reasoned method of determining exactly different amounts of Good Desert. Indeed, perhaps, Common Sense scarcely holds such a method to be possible: for though it considers Ideal Justice to consist in rewarding Desert, it regards as Utopian any general attempt to realize this ideal in the social distribution of the means of happiness. In the actual state of society it is only within a very limited range that any endeavour is made to reward Good Desert. Parents attempt this to some extent in dealing with their children, and the State in rewarding remarkable public services rendered by statesmen, soldiers, etc.: but reflection on these cases will show how very rough and imperfect are the standards used in deciding the amount due. And ordinarily the only kind of Justice which we try to realize is that which consists in the fulfilment of contracts and definite expectations; leaving the general fairness of Distribution by Bargaining to take care of itself.

7. When we pass to consider the case of Criminal Justice, we find, in the first place, difficulties corresponding to those which we have already noticed. We find, to begin, a similar implication and partial confusion of the ideas of Law and Justice. For, as was said, by 'bringing a man to Justice' we commonly mean 'inflicting legal punishment' on him: and we think it right that neither more nor less than the penalty prescribed by law should be executed, even though we may regard the legal scale of punishment as unjust. At the same time, we have no such perplexity in respect of changes in the law as occurs in the case of Civil Justice; for we do not think that a man can acquire, by custom, prescriptive rights to over-lenient punishment, as he is thought to do to an unequal distribution of liberties and privileges. If now we investigate the ideal of Criminal Justice, as intuitively determined, we certainly find that in so far as

punishment is not regarded as merely preventive, it is commonly thought that it ought to be proportioned to the gravity of crime. Still, when we endeavour to make the method of apportionment perfectly rational and precise, the difficulties seem at least as great as in the case of Good Desert. For, first, the assumption of Free Will seems necessarily to come in here also; since if a man's bad deeds are entirely caused by nature and circumstances, it certainly appears, as Robert Owen urged, that he does not properly deserve to be punished for them; Justice would rather seem to require us to try to alter the conditions under which he acts. And we actually do punish deliberate offences more than impulsive, perhaps as implying a more free choice of evil. Again, we think that offences committed by persons who have had no moral training, or a perverted training, are really less criminal; at the same time it is commonly agreed that men can hardly remit punishment on this account. Again the gravity—from a moral point of view—of a crime seems to be at least much reduced, if the motive be laudable, as when a man kills a villain whose crimes elude legal punishment, or heads a hopeless rebellion for the good of his country: still it would be paradoxical to affirm that we ought to reduce punishment proportionally: Common Sense would hold that—whatever God may do—men must, generally speaking, inflict severe punishment for any gravely mischievous act forbidden by law which has been intentionally done, even though it may have been prompted by a good motive.

But even if we neglect the motive, and take the intention only into account, it is not easy to state clear principles for determining the gravity of crimes. For sometimes, as in the case of the patriotic rebel, the intention of the criminal is to do what is right and good: and in many cases, though he knows that he is doing wrong, he does not intend to cause any actual harm to any sentient being; as when a thief takes what he thinks will not be missed. Again, we do not commonly think that a crime is rendered less grave by being kept perfectly secret; and yet a great part of the harm done by a crime is the 'secondary evil' (as Bentham calls it) of the alarm and insecurity which it causes; and this part is cut off by complete secrecy. It may be replied that this latter difficulty is not a practical one; because we are not called upon to punish a crime until it has been discovered, and then the secondary evil has been caused, and is all the greater because of the previous secrecy. But it remains true that it was not designed for discovery; and therefore that this part of the evil caused by the crime was not intended by the criminal. And if we say that the heinousness of the crime depends on the loss of happiness that would generally be caused by such acts if they were allowed to go unpunished, and that we must suppose the criminal to be aware of this; we seem to be endeavouring to force a utilitarian theory into an intuitional form by means of a legal fiction.

We have hitherto spoken of intentional wrong-doing: but positive law awards punishment also for harm that is due to rashness or negligence; and the justification of this involves us in further difficulties. Some jurists seem to regard rashness and negligence as positive states of mind, in which the agent consciously refuses the attention or reflection which he knows he ought to give; and no doubt this sort of wilful recklessness does sometimes occur, and seems as properly punishable as if the resulting harm had been positively intended. But the law as actually administered does not require evidence that this was the agent's state of mind (which indeed in most cases it would be impossible to give): but is content with proof that the harm might have been prevented by such care as an average man would have shown under the circumstances. And most commonly by 'carelessness' we simply mean a purely negative psychological fact, i.e. that the agent did not perform certain processes of observation or reflection; it is therefore at the time strictly involuntary, and so scarcely seems to involve ill-desert. It may be said perhaps that though the present carelessness is not blameworthy, the past neglect to cultivate habits of care is so. But in many individual instances we cannot reasonably infer even this past neglect; and in such cases the utilitarian theory of punishment, which regards it as a means of preventing similar harmful acts in the future, seems alone applicable. Similar difficulties arise, as was before hinted, in determining the limits within which Reparation is due; that is, on the view that it is not incumbent on us to make compensation for all harm caused by our muscular actions, but only for harm which—if not intentional—was due to our rashness or negligence.

The results of this examination of Justice may be summed up as follows. The prominent element in Justice as ordinarily conceived is a kind of Equality: that is, Impartiality in the observance or enforcement of certain general rules allotting good or evil to individuals. But when we have clearly distinguished this element, we see that the definition of the virtue required for practical guidance is left obviously incomplete.

Inquiring further for the right general principles of distribution, we find that our common notion of Justice includes—besides the principle of Reparation for injury—two quite distinct and divergent elements. The one, which we may call Conservative Justice, is realized (1) in the observance of Law and Contracts and definite understandings, and in the enforcement of such penalties for the violation of these as have been legally determined and announced; and (2) in the fulfilment of natural and normal expectations. This latter obligation, however, is of a somewhat indefinite kind. But the other element, which we have called Ideal Justice, is still more difficult to define; for there seem to be two quite distinct conceptions of it, embodied respectively in what we have called the Individualistic and the Socialistic Ideals of a political community. The first of these takes the realization of Freedom as the ultimate end and standard of right social relations: but on examining it closer we find that the notion of Freedom will not give a practicable basis for social construction without certain arbitrary definitions and limitations: and even if we admit these, still a society in which Freedom is realised as far as is feasible does not completely suit our sense of Justice. *Prima facie,* this is more satisfied by the Socialistic Ideal of Distribution, founded on the principle of requiting Desert: but when we try to make this principle precise, we find ourselves again involved in grave difficulties; and similar perplexities beset the working out of rules of Criminal Justice on the same principle.

The Utilitarian Theory of Justice

HENRY SIDGWICK

. . . "That Justice is useful to society," says Hume, "it would be a superfluous undertaking to prove": what he endeavours to show at some length is "that public utility is the *sole* origin of Justice": and the same question of origin has occupied the chief attention of J. S. Mill. Here, however, we are not so much concerned with the growth of the sentiment of Justice from experiences of utility, as with the Utilitarian basis of the mature notion; while at the same time if the analysis previously given be correct, the Justice that is commonly demanded and inculcated is something more complex than these writers have recognized. What Hume (e.g.) means by Justice is rather what I should call Order, understood in its widest sense: the observance of the actual system of rules, whether strictly legal or customary, which bind together the different members of any society into an organic whole, checking malevolent or otherwise injurious impulses, distributing the different objects of men's clashing desires, and exacting such positive services, customary or contractual, as are commonly recognized as matters of debt. And though there have rarely been wanting plausible empirical arguments for the revolutionary paradox quoted by Plato, that "laws are imposed in the interest of rulers," it remains true that the general conduciveness to social happiness of the habit of Order or Law-observance, is, as Hume says, too obvious to need proof; indeed it is of such paramount importance to a community, that even where particular laws are clearly injurious it is usually expedient to observe them, apart from any penalty which their breach might entail on the individual. We saw, however, that Common Sense sometimes bids us refuse obedience to bad laws, because "we ought to obey God rather than men" (though there seems to be no clear intuition as to the kind or degree of badness that justifies resistance); and further allows us, in special emergencies, to

From Chapter III, Book IV, of Sidgwick's *The Methods of Ethics*.

violate rules generally good, for "necessity has no law," and "salus populi suprema lex."

These and similar common opinions seem at least to suggest that the limits of the duty of Law-observance are to be determined by utilitarian considerations. While, again, the Utilitarian view gets rid of the difficulties in which the attempt to define intuitively the truly legitimate source of legislative authority involved us; at the same time that it justifies to some extent each of the different views current as to the intrinsic legitimacy of governments. For, on the one hand, it finds the moral basis of any established political order primarily in its effects rather than its causes; so that, generally speaking, obedience will seem due to any *de facto* government that is not governing very badly. On the other hand, in so far as laws originating in a particular way are likely to be (1) better, or (2) more readily observed, it is a Utilitarian duty to aim at introducing this mode of origination: and thus in a certain stage of social development it may be right that (e.g.) a 'representative system' should be popularly demanded, or possibly (in extreme cases) even introduced by force: while, again, there is expediency in maintaining an ancient mode of legislation, because men readily obey such: and loyalty to a dispossessed government may be on the whole expedient, even at the cost of some temporary suffering and disorder, in order that ambitious men may not find usurpation too easy. Here, as elsewhere, Utilitarianism at once supports the different reasons commonly put forward as absolute, and also brings them theoretically to a common measure, so that in any particular case we have a principle of decision between conflicting political arguments.

As was before said, this Law-observance, in so far at least as it affects the interests of other individuals, is what we frequently mean by Justice. It seems, however, that the notion of Justice, exhaustively analysed, includes several distinct elements combined in a somewhat complex manner: we have to inquire, therefore, what latent utilities are represented by each of these elements.

Now, first, a constant part of the notion, which appears in it even when the Just is not distinguished from the Legal, is impartiality or the negation of arbitrary inequality. This impartiality, as we saw (whether exhibited in the establishment or in the administration of laws), is merely a special application of the wider maxim that it cannot be right to treat two persons differently if their cases are similar in all material circumstances. And Utilitarianism, as we saw, admits this maxim no less than other systems of Ethics. At the same time, this negative criterion is clearly inadequate for the complete determination of what is just in laws, or in conduct generally; when we have admitted this, it still remains to ask, "What are the inequalities in laws, and in the distribution of pleasures and pains outside the sphere of law, which are not arbitrary and unreasonable? and to what general principles can they be reduced?"

Here in the first place we may explain, on utilitarian principles, why apparently arbitrary inequality in a certain part of the conduct of individuals is not regarded as injustice or even—in some cases—as in any way censurable. For freedom of action is an important source of happiness to the agents, and a socially useful stimulus to their energies: hence it is obviously expedient that a man's free choice in the distribution of wealth or kind services should not be restrained by the fear of legal penalties, or even of social disapprobation, beyond what the interests of others clearly require; and therefore, when distinctly recognized claims are satisfied, it is *pro tanto* expedient that the mere preferences of an individual should be treated by others as legitimate grounds for inequality in the distribution of his property or services. Nay, as we have before seen, it is within certain limits expedient that each individual should practically regard his own unreasoned impulses as reasonable grounds of action: as in the rendering of services prompted by such affections as are normally and properly spontaneous and unforced.

Passing to consider the general principles upon which 'just claims' as commonly recognized appear to be based, we notice that the grounds of a number of such claims may be brought under the general head of 'normal expectations': but that the stringency of such obligations varies much in degree, according as the expectations are based upon definite engagements, or on some vague mutual understanding, or are merely such as an average man would form from past experience of the conduct of other men. In these latter cases Common Sense appeared to be somewhat perplexed as to the validity of the claims. But for the Utilitarian the difficulty has ceased to exist. He will hold any disappointment of expectations to be *pro tanto* an evil, but a greater evil in proportion to the previous security of the expectant individual, from the greater shock thus given to his reliance on the conduct of his fellow-men generally: and many times greater in proportion as the expectation is generally recognized as normal and reasonable, as in this case the shock extends to all who are in any way cognisant of his disappointment. The importance to mankind of being able to rely on each other's actions is so great, that in ordinary cases of absolutely definite engagements there is scarcely any advantage that can counterbalance the harm done by violating them. Still, we found that several exceptions and qualifications to the rule of Good Faith were more or less distinctly recognized by Common Sense: and most of these have a utilitarian basis, which it does not need much penetration to discern. To begin, we may notice that the superficial view of the obligation of a promise which makes it depend on the assertion of the promiser, and not, as Utilitarians hold, on the expectations produced in the promisee, cannot fairly be attributed to Common Sense: which certainly condemns a breach of promise much more strongly when others have acted in reliance on it, than when its observance did not directly concern others, so that its breach involves for them only the indirect evil of a bad precedent—as when a man breaks a pledge of total abstinence. We see, again, how the utilitarian reasons for keeping a promise are diminished by a material change of circumstances, for in that case the expectations disappointed by breaking it are at least not those which the promise originally created. It is obvious, too, that it is a disadvantage to the community that men should be able to rely on the performance of promises procured by fraud or unlawful force, so far as encouragement is thereby given to the use of fraud or force for this end. We saw, again, that when the performance would be injurious to the promisee, Common Sense is disposed to admit that its obligation is superseded; and is at least doubtful whether the promise should be kept, even when it is only the promiser who would be injured, if the harm be extreme—both which qualifications are in harmony with Utilitarianism. And similarly for the other qualifications and exceptions: they all turn out to be as clearly utilitarian, as the general utility of keeping one's word is plain and manifest.

But further, the expediency of satisfying normal expectations, even when they are not based upon a definite contract, is undeniable; it will clearly conduce to the tranquillity of social existence, and to the settled and well-adjusted activity on which social happiness greatly depends, that such expectations should be as little as possible baulked. And here Utilitarianism relieves us of the difficulties which beset the common view of just conduct as something absolutely precise and definite For in this vaguer region we cannot draw a sharp line between valid and invalid claims; 'injustice' shades gradually off into mere 'hardship.' Hence the Utilitarian view that the disappointment of natural expectations is an evil, but an evil which must sometimes be incurred for the sake of a greater good, is that to which Common Sense is practically forced, though unable to reconcile it with the theoretical absoluteness of Intuitive Morality.

The gain of recognizing the relativity of this obligation will be still more felt, when we consider what I distinguished as Ideal Justice, and examine the general conceptions of this which we find expressed or latent in current criticisms of the existing order of Society.

We have seen that there are two competing views of an ideally just social order—or perhaps we may say two extreme types between which the looser notions of ordinary men seem to fluctuate—which I called respectively Individualistic and Socialistic. According to the former view an ideal system of Law ought to aim at Freedom, or perfect mutual non-interference of all the members of the community, as an absolute end. Now the general utilitarian reasons for leaving each rational adult free to seek happiness in his own way are obvious and striking; for, generally speaking, each is best qualified to provide for his own interests, since even when he does not know best what they are and how to attain them, he is at any rate most keenly concerned for them: and again, the consciousness of freedom and concomitant responsibility increases the average effective activity of men: and besides the discomfort of constraint is directly an evil and *pro tanto* to be avoided. Still, we saw that the attempt to construct a consistent code of laws, taking Maximum Freedom (instead of Happiness) as an absolute end, must lead to startling paradoxes and insoluble puzzles: and in fact the practical interpretation of the notion 'Freedom,' and the limits within which its realization has been actually sought, have always—even in the freest societies—been more or less consciously determined by considerations of expediency. So that we may fairly say that in so far as Common Sense has adopted the Individualistic ideal in politics, it has always been as subordinate to and limited by the Utilitarian first principle.

It seems, however, that what we commonly demand or long for, under the name of Ideal Justice, is not so much the realization of Freedom, as the distribution of good and evil according to Desert: indeed it is as a means to this latter end that Freedom is often advocated; for it is said that if we protect men completely from mutual interference, each will reap the good and bad consequences of his own conduct, and so be happy or unhappy in proportion to his deserts. In particular, it has been widely held that if a free exchange of wealth and services is allowed, each individual will obtain from society, in money or other advantages, what his services are really worth. We saw, however, that the price which an individual obtains under a system of perfect free trade, for wealth or services exchanged by him, may for several reasons be not proportioned to the social utility of what he exchanges: and reflective Common Sense seems to admit this disproportion as to some extent legitimate, under the influence of utilitarian considerations correcting the unreflective utterances of moral sentiments.

To take a particular case: if a moral man were asked how far it is right to take advantage in bargaining of another's ignorance, probably his first impulse would be to condemn such a procedure altogether. But reflection, I think, would show him that such a censure would be too sweeping: that it would be contrary to Common Sense to "blame A for having, in negotiating with a stranger B, taken advantage of B's ignorance of facts known to himself, provided that A's superior knowledge had been obtained by a legitimate use of diligence and foresight, which B might have used with equal success. . . . What prevents us from censuring in this and similar cases is, I conceive, a more or less conscious apprehension of the indefinite loss to the wealth of the community that is likely to result from any effective social restrictions on the free pursuit and exercise" of economic knowledge. And for somewhat similar reasons of general expediency, if the question be raised whether it is fair for a class of persons to gain by the unfavourable economic situation of any class with which they deal, Common Sense at least hesitates to censure such gains—at any rate when such unfavourable situation is due "to the gradual action of general causes, for the existence of which the persons who gain are not specially responsible."

The general principle of 'requiting good desert,' so far as Common Sense really accepts it as practically applicable to the relations of men in society, is broadly in harmony with Utilitarianism; since we obviously encourage the production of general happiness by rewarding men for felicific conduct; only the Utilitarian scale of rewards will not be determined entirely by the magnitude of the services performed, but partly also by the difficulty of inducing men to perform them. But this latter element seems to be always taken into account (though perhaps unconsciously) by Common Sense: for, as we have been led to notice, we do not commonly recognize merit in right actions, if they are such as men are naturally inclined to perform rather too much than too little. Again, in cases where the Intuitional principle that ill-desert lies in wrong intention conflicts with the Utilitarian view of punishment as purely preventive, we find that in the actual administration of criminal justice, Common Sense is forced, however reluctantly, into practical agreement with Utilitarianism. Thus after a civil war it demands the execution of the most purely patriotic rebels; and after a railway accident it clamours for the severe punishment of unintentional neglects, which, except for their consequences, would have been regarded as very venial.

If, however, in any distribution of pleasures and privileges, or of pains and burdens, considerations of desert do not properly come in (*i.e.* if the good or evil to be distributed have no relation to any conduct on the part of the persons who are to receive either)—or if it is practically impossible to take such considerations into account—then Common Sense seems to fall back on simple equality as the principle of just apportionment.[1] And we have seen that the Utilitarian, in the case supposed, will reasonably accept Equality as the only mode of distribution that is not arbitrary; and it may be observed that this mode of apportioning the means of happiness is likely to produce more happiness on the whole, not only because men have a disinterested aversion to unreason, but still more because they have an aversion to any kind of inferiority to others, which is much intensified when the inferiority seems unreasonable. This latter feeling is so strong that it often prevails in spite of obvious claims of desert; and it may even be sometimes expedient that it should so prevail.

For, finally, it must be observed that Utilitarianism furnishes us with a common standard to which the different elements included in the notion of Justice may be reduced. Such a standard is imperatively required: as these different elements are continually liable to conflict with each other. The issue, for example, in practical politics between Con-

---

[1] I have before observed that it is quite in harmony with Utilitarian principles to recognize a sphere of private conduct within which each individual may distribute his wealth and kind services as unequally as he chooses, without incurring censure as unjust.

servatives and Reformers often represents such a conflict: the question is, whether we ought to do a certain violence to expectations arising naturally out of the existing social order, with the view of bringing about a distribution of the means of happiness more in accordance with ideal justice. Here, if my analysis of the common notion of Justice be sound, the attempt to extract from it a clear decision of such an issue must necessarily fail: as the conflict is, so to say, permanently latent in the very core of Common Sense. But the Utilitarian will merely use this notion of Justice as a guide to different kinds of utilities; and in so far as these are incompatible, he will balance one set of advantages against the other, and decide according to the preponderance.

Part Two

Criticism and

Revision of the

Utilitarian Theory of Justice

Punishment

J. D. MABBOTT

I propose in this paper to defend a retributive theory of punishment and to reject absolutely all utilitarian considerations from its justification. I feel sure that this enterprise must arouse deep suspicion and hostility both among philosophers (who must have felt that the retributive view is the only moral theory except perhaps psychological hedonism which has been definitely destroyed by criticism) and among practical men (who have welcomed its steady decline in our penal practice).

The question I am asking is this. Under what circumstances is the punishment of some particular person justified and why? The theories of reform and deterrence which are usually considered to be the only alternatives to retribution involve well-known difficulties. These are considered fully and fairly in Dr. Ewing's book, *The Morality of Punishment,* and I need not spend long over them. The central difficulty is that both would on occasion justify the punishment of an innocent man, the deterrent theory if he were believed to have been guilty by those likely to commit the crime in future, and the reformatory theory if he were a bad man though not a criminal. To this may be added the point against the deterrent theory that it is the threat of punishment and not punishment itself which deters, and that when deterrence seems to de-

Reprinted from *Mind,* vol. 49 (1939) by permission of the author and the Editor.

pend on actual punishment, to implement the threat, it really depends on publication and may be achieved if men believe that punishment has occurred even if in fact it has not. As Bentham saw, for a Utilitarian apparent justice is everything, real justice is irrelevant.

Dr. Ewing and other moralists would be inclined to compromise with retribution in the face of the above difficulties. They would admit that one fact and one fact only can justify the punishment of this man, and that is a *past* fact, that he has committed a crime. To this extent reform and deterrence theories, which look only to the consequences, are wrong. But they would add that retribution can determine only *that* a man should be punished. It cannot determine how or how much, and here reform and deterrence may come in. Even Bradley, the fiercest retributionist of modern times, says "Having once the right to punish we may modify the punishment according to the useful and the pleasant, but these are external to the matter; they cannot give us a right to punish and nothing can do that but criminal desert." Dr. Ewing would maintain that the whole estimate of the amount and nature of a punishment may be effected by considerations of reform and deterrence. It seems to me that this is a surrender which the upholders of retribution dare not make. As I said above, it is publicity and not punishment which deters, and the publicity though often spoken of as "part of a man's punishment" is no more part of it than his arrest or his detention prior to trial, though both these may be also unpleasant and bring him into disrepute. A judge sentences a man to three years' imprisonment not to three years *plus* three columns in the press. Similarly with reform. The visit of the prison chaplain is not part of a man's punishment nor is the visit of Miss Fields or Mickey Mouse.

The truth is that while punishing a man and punishing him justly, it is possible to deter others, and also to attempt to reform him, and if these additional goods are achieved the total state of affairs is better than it would be with the just punishment alone. But reform and deterrence are not modifications of the punishment, still less reasons for it. A parallel may be found in the case of tact and truth. If you have to tell a friend an unpleasant truth you may do all you can to put him at his ease and spare his feelings as much as possible, while still making sure that he understands your meaning. In such a case no one would say that your offer of a cigarette beforehand or your apology afterwards are modifications of the truth still less reasons for telling it. You do not tell the truth in order to spare his feelings, but having to tell the truth you also spare his feelings. So Bradley was right when he said that reform and deterrence were "external to the matter," but therefore wrong when he said that they may "modify the punishment." Reporters are admitted to our trials so that punishments may become public and help to deter others. But the punishment would be no less just were reporters excluded and deterrence not achieved. Prison authorities may make it possible that a convict may become physically or morally better. They cannot ensure either result; and the punishment would still be just if the criminal took no advantage of their arrangements and their efforts failed. Some moralists see this and exclude these "extra" arrangements for deterrence and reform. They say that it must be the punishment *itself* which reforms and deters. But it is just my point that the punishment *itself* seldom reforms the criminal and never deters others. It is only "extra" arrangements which have any chance of achieving either result. As this is the central point of my paper, at the cost of laboured repetition I would ask the upholders of reform and deterrence two questions. Suppose it could be shown that a particular criminal had not been improved by a punishment and also that no other would-be criminal had been deterred by it, would that prove that the punishment was unjust? Suppose it were discovered that a particular criminal had lived a much better life after his release and that many would-be criminals believing him to have been guilty were influenced by his fate, but yet that the "criminal" was punished for something he had never done, would these excellent results prove the punishment just?

It will be observed that I have throughout treated punishment as a purely legal matter. A "criminal" means a man who has broken a law, not a bad man; an "innocent" man is a man who has not broken the law in connection with which he is being punished, though he may be a bad man and have broken other laws. Here I dissent from most upholders of the retributive theory—from Hegel, from Bradley, and from Dr. Ross. They maintain that the essential connection is one between punishment and moral or social wrong-doing.

My fundamental difficulty with their theory is the question of *status*. It takes two to make a punishment, and for a moral or social wrong I can find no punisher. We may be tempted to say when we hear of some brutal action "that ought to be punished"; but I cannot see how there can be duties which are nobody's duties. If I see a man ill-treating a horse in a country where cruelty to animals is not a legal offence, and I say to him "I shall now punish you," he will reply, rightly, "What has it to do with you? Who made you a judge and a ruler over me?" I may have a duty to try to stop him and one way of stopping him may be to hit him, but another way may be to buy the horse. Neither the blow nor the price is a punishment. For a moral offence, God alone has the *status* necessary to punish the offender; and the theologians are becoming more and more doubtful whether even God has a duty to punish wrong-doing.

Dr. Ross would hold that not all wrong-doing is punishable, but only invasion of the rights of others; and in such a case it might be thought that the injured party had a right to punish. His right, however, is rather a right to reparation, and should not be confused with punishment proper.

This connection, on which I insist, between punishment and crime, not between punishment and moral or social wrong, alone accounts for some of our beliefs about punishment, and also meets many objections to the retributive theory as stated in its ordinary form. The first point on which it helps us is with regard to retrospective legislation. Our objection to this practice is unaccountable on reform and deterrence theories. For a man who commits a wrong before the date on which a law against it is passed, is as much in need of reform as a man who commits it afterwards; nor is deterrence likely to suffer because of additional punishments for the same offence. But the orthodox retributive theory is equally at a loss here, for if punishment is given for moral wrong-doing or for invasion of the rights of others, that immorality or invasion existed as certainly before the passing of the law as after it.

My theory also explains, where it seems to me all others do not, the case of punishment imposed by an authority who believes the law in question is a bad law. I was myself for some time disciplinary officer of a college whose rules included a rule compelling attendance at chapel. Many of those who broke this rule broke it on principle. I punished them. I certainly did not want to reform them; I respected their characters and their views. I certainly did not want to drive others into chapel through fear of penalties. Nor did I think there had been a wrong done which merited retribution. I wished I could have believed that I would have done the same myself. My position was clear. They had broken a rule; they knew it and I knew it. Nothing more was necessary to make punishment proper.

I know that the usual answer to this is that the judge enforces a bad law because otherwise law in general would suffer and good laws would be broken. The effect of punishing good men for breaking bad laws is that fewer bad men break good laws.

[*Excursus on Indirect Utilitarianism.* The above argument is a particular instance of a general utilitarian solution of all similar problems. When I am in funds and consider whether I should pay my debts or give the same amount to charity, I must choose the former because repayment not only benefits my creditor (for the benefit to him might be less than the good done through charity) but also upholds the general credit system. I tell the truth when a lie might do more good to the parties directly concerned, because I thus increase general trust and confidence. I keep a promise when it might do more immediate good to break it, because indirectly I bring it about that promises will be more readily made in future and this will outweigh the immediate loss involved. Dr. Ross has pointed out that the effect on the credit system of my refusal to pay a debt is greatly exaggerated. But I have a more serious objection of principle. It is that in all these cases the indirect effects do not result from my wrong action—my lie or defalcation or bad faith—but from the publication of these actions. If in any instance the breaking of the rule were to remain unknown then I could consider only the direct or immediate consequences. Thus in my "compulsory chapel" case I could have considered which of my culprits were law-abiding men generally and unlikely to break any other college rule. Then I could have sent for each of these separately and said "I shall let you off if you will tell no one I have done so." By these means the general keeping of rules would not have suffered. Would this course have been correct? It must be remembered that the proceedings need not deceive everybody. So long as they deceive would-be law-breakers the good is achieved.

As this point is of crucial importance and as it has an interest beyond the immediate issue, and gives a clue to what I regard as the true general nature of law and punishment, I may be excused for expanding and illustrating it by an example or two from other fields. Dr. Ross says that two men dying on a desert island would have duties to keep promises to each other even though their breaking them would not affect the future general confidence in promises at all. Here is certainly the same point. But as I find that desert-island morality always rouses suspicion among ordinary men I should like to quote two instances from my own experience which also illustrate the problem.

(i) A man alone with his father at his death promises him a private and quiet funeral. He finds later that both directly and indirectly the keeping of this promise will cause pain and misunderstanding. He can see no particular positive good that the quiet funeral will achieve. No one yet knows that he has made the promise nor need anyone ever know. Should he therefore act as though it had never been made?

(ii) A college has a fund given to it for the encouragement of a subject which is now expiring. Other expanding subjects are in great need of endowment. Should the authorities divert the money? Those who oppose the diversion have previously stood on the past, the promise. But one day one of them discovers the "real reason" for this slavery to a dead donor. He says "We must consider not only the value of this money for these purposes, since on all direct consequences it should be diverted at once. We must remember the effect of this diversion on the general system of benefactions. We know that benefactors like to endow special objects, and this act of ours would discourage such benefactors in future and leave learning worse off." Here again is the indirect utilitarian reason for choosing the alternative which direct utilitarianism would reject. But the immediate answer to this from the most ingenious member of the opposition was crushing and final. He said, "Divert the money but keep it dark." This is obviously correct. It is not the act of diversion which would diminish the stream of benefactions but the news of it reaching the ears of benefactors. Provided that no possible benefactor got to hear of it no indirect loss would result. But the justification of our action would depend entirely on the success of the measures for "keeping it dark." I remember how I felt and how others felt that whatever answer was right this result was certainly wrong. But it follows that indirect utilitarianism is wrong in all such cases. For its argument can always be met by "Keep it dark."]

The view, then, that a judge upholds a bad law in order that law in general should not suffer is indefensible. He upholds it simply because he has no right to dispense from punishment.

The connection of punishment with law-breaking and not with wrong-doing also escapes moral objections to the retributive theory as held by Kant and Hegel or by Bradley and Ross. It is asked how we can measure moral wrong or balance it with pain, and how pain can wipe out moral wrong. Retributivists have been pushed into holding that pain *ipso facto* represses the worse self and frees the better, when this is contrary to the vast majority of observed cases. But if punishment is not intended to measure or balance or negate moral wrong then all this is beside the mark. There is the further difficulty of reconciling punishment with repentance and with forgiveness. Repentance is the reaction morally appropriate to moral wrong and punishment added to remorse is an unnecessary evil. But if punishment is associated with law-breaking and not with moral evil the punisher is not entitled to consider whether the criminal is penitent any more than he may consider whether the law is good. So, too, with forgiveness. Forgiveness is not appropriate to law-breaking. (It is noteworthy that when, in divorce cases, the law has to recognize forgiveness it calls it "condonation," which is symptomatic of the difference of attitude.) Nor is forgiveness appropriate to moral evil. It is appropriate to personal injury. No one has any right to forgive me except the person I have injured. No judge or jury can do so. But the person I have injured has no right to punish me. Therefore there is no clash between punishment and forgiveness since these two duties do not fall on the same person nor in connection with the same characteristic of my act. (It is the weakness of vendetta that it tends to confuse this clear line, though even there it is only by personifying the family that the injured party and the avenger are identified. Similarly we must guard against the plausible fallacy of personifying society and regarding the criminal as "injuring society," for then once more the old dilemma about forgiveness would be insoluble.) A clergyman friend of mine catching a burglar red-handed was puzzled about his duty. In the end he ensured the man's punishment by information and evidence, and at the same time showed his own forgiveness by visiting the man in prison and employing him when he came out. I believe any "good Christian" would accept this as representing his duty. But obviously if the punishment is thought of as imposed *by* the victim or *for* the injury or immorality then the contradiction with forgiveness is hopeless.

So far as the question of the actual punishment of any individual is concerned this paper could stop here. No punishment is morally retributive or reformative or deterrent. Any criminal punished for any

one of these reasons is certainly unjustly punished. The only justification for punishing any man is that he has broken a law.

In a book which has already left its mark on prison administration I
have found a criminal himself confirming these views. *Walls Have
Mouths*, by W. F. R. Macartney, is prefaced, and provided with ap-
pendices to each chapter, by Compton Mackenzie. It is interesting to
notice how the novelist maintains that the proper object of penal
servitude should be reformation,[1] whereas the prisoner himself accepts
the view I have set out above. Macartney says "To punish a man is to
treat him as an equal. To be punished *for an offence against rules* is a
sane man's right."[2] It is striking also that he never uses "injustice" to
describe the brutality or provocation which he experienced. He makes
it clear that there were only two types of prisoner who were *unjustly*
imprisoned, those who were insane and not responsible for the acts
for which they were punished[3] and those who were innocent and had
broken no law.[4] It is irrelevant, as he rightly observes, that some of these
innocent men were, like Steinie Morrison, dangerous and violent characters, who on utilitarian grounds might well have been restrained. That
made their punishment no whit less unjust.[5] To these general types may
be added two specific instances of injustice. First, the sentences on the
Dartmoor mutineers. "The Penal Servitude Act . . . lays down specific
punishments for mutiny and incitement to mutiny, which include flog-
ging. . . . Yet on the occasion of the only big mutiny in an English
prison, men are not dealt with by the Act specially passed to meet
mutiny in prison, but are taken out of gaol and tried under an Act
expressly passed to curb and curtail the Chartists—a revolutionary movement."[6] Here again the injustice does not lie in the actual effect the
sentences are likely to have on the prisoners (though Macartney has
some searching suggestions about that also) but in condemning men
for breaking a law they did not break and not for breaking the law
they did break. The second specific instance is that of Coulton, who
served his twenty years and then was brought back to prison to do
another eight years and to die. This is due to the "unjust order that no
lifer shall be released unless he has either relations or a job to whom
he can go: and it is actually suggested that this is really for the lifer's
own good. Just fancy, you admit that the man in doing years upon years

---

[1] p. 97. [2] p. 165. My italics. [3] pp. 165-166. [4] p. 298.
[5] p. 301. [6] p. 255.

in prison had expiated his crime: but, instead of releasing him, you keep him a further time—perhaps another three years—because you say he has nowhere to go. Better a ditch and hedge than prison! True, there are abnormal cases who want to stay in prison, but Lawrence wanted to be a private soldier, and men go into monasteries. Because occasionally a man wants to stay in prison, must every lifer who has lost his family during his sentence (I was doing only ten years and I lost all my family) be kept indefinitely in gaol after he has paid his debt?" [7] Why is it unjust? Because he has paid his debt. When that is over it is for the man himself to decide what is for his own good. Once again the reform and utilitarian arguments are summarily swept aside. Injustice lies not in bad treatment or treatment which is not in the man's own interest, but in restriction which, according to the law, he has not merited.

It is true that Macartney writes, in one place, a paragraph of general reflection on punishment in which he confuses, as does Compton Mackenzie, retribution with revenge and in which he seems to hold that the retributive theory has some peculiar connection with private property. "Indeed it is difficult to see how, in society as it is to-day constituted, a humane prison system could function. All property is sacred, although the proceeds of property may well be reprehensible, therefore any offence against property is sacrilege and must be punished. Till a system eventuates which is based not on exploitation of man by man and class by class, prisons must be dreadful places, but at least there might be an effort to ameliorate the more savage side of the retaliation, and this could be done very easily." [8] The alternative system of which no doubt he is thinking is the Russian system described in his quotations from *A Physician's Tour in Soviet Russia*, by Sir James Purves-Stewart, the system of "correctional colonies" providing curative "treatment" for the different types of criminal.[9] There are two confusions here, to one of which we shall return later. First, Macartney confuses the retributive system with the punishment of one particular type of crime, offences against property, when he must have known that the majority of offenders against property do not find themselves in Dartmoor or even in Wandsworth. After all his own offence was not one against property—it was traffic with a foreign Power—and it was one for which in the classless society of Russia the punishment is death. It is surely clear that a retributive system may be adopted for any class of crime. Secondly, Macartney

[7] p. 400. [8] pp. 166, 167. [9] p. 229.

confuses injustice within a penal system with the wrongfulness of a
penal system. When he pleads for "humane prisons" as if the essence of
the prison should be humanity, or when Compton Mackenzie says the
object of penal servitude should be reform, both of them are giving up
punishment altogether, not altering it. A Russian "correctional colony,"
if its real object is curative treatment, is no more a "prison" than is an
isolation hospital or a lunatic asylum. To this distinction between
abolishing injustice in punishment and abolishing punishment altogether we must now turn.

It will be objected that my original question "Why ought X to be
punished?" is an illegitimate isolation of the issue. I have treated the
whole set of circumstances as determined. X is a citizen of a state. About
his citizenship, whether willing or unwilling, I have asked no questions.
About the government, whether it is good or bad, I do not enquire. X
has broken a law. Concerning the law, whether it is well-devised or not,
I have not asked. Yet all these questions are surely relevant before it
can be decided whether a particular punishment is just. It is the essence
of my position that none of these questions is relevant. Punishment is a
corollary of law-breaking by a member of the society whose law is broken.
This is a static and an abstract view but I see no escape from it. Considerations of utility come in on two quite different issues. Should there
be laws, and what laws should there be? As a legislator I may ask what
general types of action would benefit the community, and, among these,
which can be "standardized" without loss, or should be standardized to
achieve their full value. This, however, is not the primary question since
particular laws may be altered or repealed. The choice which is the
essential *prius* of punishment is the choice that there should be laws.
The choice is not Hobson's. Other methods may be considered. A government might attempt to standardize certain modes of action by means
of advice. It might proclaim its view and say "Citizens are requested"
to follow this or that procedure. Or again it might decide to deal with
each case as it arose in the manner most effective for the common
welfare. Anarchists have wavered between these two alternatives and a
third—that of doing nothing to enforce a standard of behaviour but
merely giving arbitrational decisions between conflicting parties, decisions binding only by consent.

I think it can be seen without detailed examination of particular laws
that the method of law-making has its own advantages. Its orders are

explicit and general. It makes behaviour reliable and predictable. Its threat of punishment may be so effective as to make punishment unnecessary. It promises to the good citizen a certain security in his life. When I have talked to business men about some inequity in the law of liability they have usually said "Better a bad law than no law, for then we know where we are."

Someone may say I am drawing an impossible line. I deny that punishment is utilitarian; yet now I say that punishment is a corollary of law and we decide whether to have laws and which laws to have on utilitarian grounds. And surely it is only this corollary which distinguishes law from good advice or exhortation. This is a misunderstanding. Punishment is a corollary not of law but of law-breaking. Legislators do not choose to punish. They hope no punishment will be needed. Their laws would succeed even if no punishment occurred. The criminal makes the essential choice: he "brings it on himself." Other men obey the law because they see its order is reasonable, because of inertia, because of fear. In this whole area, and it may be the major part of the state, law achieves its ends without punishment. Clearly, then, punishment is not a corollary of law.

We may return for a moment to the question of amount and nature of punishment. It may be thought that this also is automatic. The law will include its own penalties and the judge will have no option. This, however, is again an initial choice of principle. If the laws do include their own penalties then the judge has no option. But the legislature might adopt a system which left complete or partial freedom to the judge, as we do except in the case of murder. Once again, what are the merits (regardless of particular laws, still more of particular cases) of fixed penalties and variable penalties? At first sight it would seem that all the advantages are with the variable penalties; for men who have broken the same law differ widely in degree of wickedness and responsibility. When, however, we remember that punishment is not an attempt to balance moral guilt this advantage is diminished. But there are still degrees of responsibility; I do not mean degrees of freedom of will but, for instance, degrees of complicity in a crime. The danger of allowing complete freedom to the judicature in fixing penalties is not merely that it lays too heavy a tax on human nature but that it would lead to the judge expressing in his penalty the degree of his own moral aversion to the crime. Or he might tend on deterrent grounds to punish more heavily a crime which was spreading and for which temptation and opportunity were frequent. Or again on deterrent grounds he might "make examples" by punishing ten times as heavily those criminals who are detected in cases in which nine out of ten evade detection. Yet we should revolt from all such punishments if they involved punishing theft more heavily than blackmail or negligence more heavily than premeditated assault. The death penalty for sheep-stealing might have been defended on such deterrent grounds. But we should dislike equating sheep-stealing with murder. Fixed penalties enable us to draw these distinctions between crimes. It is not that we can say how much imprisonment is right for a sheep-stealer. But we can grade crimes in a rough scale and penalties in a rough scale, and keep our heaviest penalties for what are socially the most serious wrongs regardless of whether these penalties will reform the criminal or whether they are exactly what deterrence would require. The compromise of laying down maximum penalties and allowing judges freedom below these limits allows for the arguments on both sides.

To return to the main issue, the position I am defending is that it is essential to a legal system that the infliction of a particular punishment should *not* be determined by the good *that particular punishment* will do either to the criminal or to "society." In exactly the same way it is essential to a credit system that the repayment of a particular debt should not be determined by the good that particular payment will do. One may consider the merits of a legal system or of a credit system, but the acceptance of either involves the surrender of utilitarian considerations in particular cases as they arise. This is in effect admitted by Ewing in one place where he says "It is the penal system as a whole which deters and not the punishment of any individual offender."[10]

To show that the choice between a legal system and its alternatives is one we do and must make, I may quote an early work of Lenin in which he was defending the Marxist tenet that the state is bound to "wither away" with the establishment of a classless society. He considers the possible objection that some wrongs by man against man are not economic and therefore that the abolition of classes would not *ipso facto* eliminate crime. But he sticks to the thesis that these surviving crimes should not be dealt with by law and judicature. "We are not Utopians

[10] A. C. Ewing, *The Morality of Punishment* (London: Routledge and Kegan Paul, Ltd., 1929), p. 66.

and do not in the least deny the possibility and inevitability of excesses by *individual persons,* and equally the need to suppress such excesses. But for this no special machine, no special instrument of repression is needed. This will be done by the armed nation itself as simply and as readily as any crowd of civilized people even in modern society parts a pair of combatants or does not allow a woman to be outraged." [11] This alternative to law and punishment has obvious demerits. Any injury not committed in the presence of the crowd, any wrong which required skill to detect or pertinacity to bring home would go untouched. The lynching mob, which is Lenin's instrument of justice, is liable to error and easily deflected from its purpose or driven to extremes. It must be a mob, for there is to be no "machine." I do not say that no alternative machine to ours could be devised but it does seem certain that the absence of all "machines" would be intolerable. An alternative machine might be based on the view that "society" is responsible for all criminality, and a curative and protective system developed. This is the system of Butler's "Erewhon" and something like it seems to be growing up in Russia except for cases of "sedition."

We choose, then, or we acquiesce in and adopt the choice of others of, a legal system as one of our instruments for the establishment of the conditions of a good life. This choice is logically prior to and independent of the actual punishment of any particular persons or the passing of any particular laws. The legislators choose particular laws within the framework of this predetermined system. Once again a small society may illustrate the reality of these choices and the distinction between them. A Headmaster launching a new school must explicitly make both decisions. First, shall we have any rules at all? Second, what rules shall he have? The first decision is a genuine one and one of great importance. Would it not be better to have an "honour" system, by which public opinion in each house or form dealt with any offence? (This is the Lenin method.) Or would complete freedom be better? Or should he issue appeals and advice? Or should he personally deal with each malefactor individually, as the case arises, in the way most likely to improve his conduct? I can well imagine an idealistic Headmaster attempting to run a school with one of these methods or with a combination of several of them and therefore without punishment. I can even imagine that with a small school of, say, twenty pupils all open to direct personal

[11] *The State and Revolution* (Eng. trans.), p. 93. Original italics.

psychological pressure from authority and from each other, these methods involving no "rules" would work. The pupils would of course grow up without two very useful habits, the habit of having some regular habits and the habit of obeying rules. But I suspect that most Head-masters, especially those of large schools, would either decide at once, or quickly be driven, to realize that some rules were necessary. This decision would be "utilitarian" in the sense that it would be determined by consideration of consequences. The question "what rules?" would then arise and again the issue is utilitarian. What action must be regularized for the school to work efficiently? The hours of arrival and departure, for instance, in a day school. But the one choice which is now no longer open to the Headmaster is whether he shall punish those who break the rules. For if he were to try to avoid this he would in fact simply be returning to the discarded method of appeals and good advice. Yet the Headmaster does not decide to punish. The pupils make the decision there. He decides actually to have rules and to threaten, but only hypothetically, to punish. The one essential condition which makes actual punishment just is a condition he *cannot* fulfil—namely that a rule should be broken.

I shall add a final word of consolation to the practical reformer. Nothing that I have said is meant to counter any movement for "penal reform" but only to insist that none of these reforms have anything to do with punishment. The only type of reformer who can claim to be reforming the system of punishment is a follower of Lenin or of Samuel Butler who is genuinely attacking the *system* and who believes there should be no laws and no punishments. But our great British reformers have been concerned not with punishment but with its accessories. When a man is sentenced to imprisonment he is not sentenced also to partial starvation, to physical brutality, to pneumonia from damp cells and so on. And any movement which makes his food sufficient to sustain health, which counters the permanent tendency to brutality on the part of his warders, which gives him a dry or even a light and well-aired cell, is pure gain and does not touch the theory of punishment. Reformatory influences and prisoners' aid arrangements are also entirely unaffected by what I have said. I believe myself that it would be best if all such arrangements were made optional for the prisoner, so as to leave him in these cases a freedom of choice which would make it clear that they are not part of his punishment. If it is said that every such reform lessens a man's punishment, I think that is simply muddled thinking which, if it were clear, would be mere brutality. For instance, a prisoners' aid society is said to lighten his punishment, because otherwise he would suffer not merely imprisonment but also unemployment on release. But he was sentenced to imprisonment, not imprisonment *plus* unemployment. If I promise to help a friend and through special circumstances I find that keeping my promise will involve upsetting my day's work, I do not say that I really promised to help him and to ruin my day's work. And if another friend carries on my work for me I do not regard him as carrying out part of my promise, nor as stopping me from carrying it out myself. He merely removes an indirect and regrettable consequence of my keeping my promise. So with punishment. The Prisoners' Aid Society does not alter a man's punishment nor diminish it, but merely removes an indirect and regrettable consequence of it. And anyone who thinks that a criminal cannot make this distinction and will regard all the inconvenience that comes to him as punishment, need only talk to a prisoner or two to find how sharply they resent these wanton additions to a punishment which by itself they will accept as just. Macartney's chapter on "Food" in the book quoted above is a good illustration of this point, as are also his comments on Clayton's administration. "To keep a man in prison for many years at considerable expense and then to free him charged to the eyes with uncontrollable venom and hatred generated by the treatment he has received in gaol, does not appear to be sensible." Clayton "endeavoured to send a man out of prison in a reasonable state of mind. 'Well, I've done my time. They were not too bad to me. Prison is prison and not a bed of roses. Still they didn't rub it in. . . .' " [12] This "reasonable state of mind" is one in which a prisoner on release feels he has been punished but not *additionally* insulted or ill-treated. I feel convinced that penal reformers would meet with even more support if they were clear that they were *not* attempting to alter the system of punishment but to give its victims "fair play." We have no more right to starve a convict than to starve an animal. We have no more right to keep a convict in a Dartmoor cell "down which the water trickles night and day" [13] than we have to keep a child in such a place. If our reformers really want to alter the system of punishment, let them come out clearly with their alternative and preach, for instance, that no human being is responsible for any wrong-doing, that

[12] p. 152. [13] *Op. cit.,* p. 258.

all the blame is on society, that curative or protective measures should be adopted, forcibly if necessary, as they are with infection or insanity. Short of this let them admit that the essence of prison is deprivation of liberty for the breaking of law, and that deprivation of food or of health or of books is unjust. And if our sentimentalists cry "coddling of prisoners," let us ask them also to come out clearly into the open and incorporate whatever starvation and disease and brutality they think necessary *into the sentences they propose*.[14] If it is said that some prisoners will prefer such reformed prisons, with adequate food and aired cells, to the outer world, we may retort that their numbers are probably not greater than those of the masochists who like to be flogged. Yet we do not hear the same "coddling" critics suggest abolition of the lash on the grounds that some criminals may like it. Even if the abolition from our prisons of all maltreatment other than that imposed by law results in a few down-and-outs breaking a window (as O. Henry's hero did) to get a night's lodging, the country will lose less than she does by her present method of sending out her discharged convicts "charged with venom and hatred" because of the additional and unconvenanted "rubbing it in" which they have received.

I hope I have established both the theoretical importance and the practical value of distinguishing between penal reform as we know and approve it—that reform which alters the accompaniments of punishment without touching its essence—and those attacks on punishment itself which are made not only by reformers who regard criminals as irresponsible and in need of treatment, but also by every judge who announces that he is punishing a man to deter others or to protect society, and by every juryman who is moved to his decision by the moral baseness of the accused rather than by his legal guilt.

[14] "One of the minor curiosities of jail life was that they quickly provided you with a hundred worries which left you no time or energy for worrying about your sentence, long or short. . . . Rather as if you were thrown into a fire with spikes in it, and the spikes hurt you so badly that you forget about the fire. But then your punishment would *be* the spikes not the fire. Why did they pretend it was only the fire, when they knew very well about the spikes?" (From *Lifer* by Jim Phelan, p. 40.)

Utilitarianism, Universalisation, and Our Duty to Be Just

JONATHAN HARRISON

In considering what common interest requires, we are, besides the immediate effects of actions, to consider what their general tendencies are, what they open the way to, and what would actually be the consequences if all were to act alike. If under the pretence of greater indigence, superfluity to the owner, or intention to give to a worthier person, I may take away a man's property, or adjudge it from him in a court of justice; another or all, in the same circumstances may do so; and thus the boundaries of property would be overthrown, and general anarchy, distrust and savageness be introduced.——
Richard Price.[1]

According to Utilitarianism, it is often said, an action is right if it produces at least as much good as any other action which the agent could have done in the circumstances in which he was placed. Besides being right, it is also a duty, if it produces more good than any other action that the agent could have done. When we are faced with a situation in which we have to choose between a number of actions, each of which would produce as much good or more than anything else we could do, but of none of which is it true that they would produce more good than anything else we could do, then we have not a duty to perform any particular one of these actions to the exclusion of the others. What is our duty is to do one or other of these actions; but it is a matter of indifference which of them we do, and we have done our duty, whichever one of them we perform.[2]

From the *Proceedings of the Aristotelian Society*, vol. 52 (1952-53). Reprinted by permission of the author and of the Aristotelian Society.
[1] Richard Price: *A Review of the Principal Questions in Morals*, edited by D. Daiches Raphael, p. 164.
[2] See G. E. Moore: *Ethics*, pp. 32-35. The definition of utilitarianism used here would not have satisfied Professor Moore, but it will do for our purposes.

There are, therefore, some right actions which are not duties, and so the words "right" and "a duty" cannot mean the same thing. This fact has been regarded as unimportant,[3] because it has been supposed that the circumstances in which we are faced with a choice between a number of right actions, none of which are duties, occur but seldom.

However, it seems to me that such situations, so far from being rare, are arising all the time. At any moment of the day, when I am not engaged in doing anything in particular, there are at least half a dozen actions I can think of which I could do, which it would be perfectly right for me to do, but none of which could, by any stretch of the imagination, be said to be duties. It is often supposed that, in such circumstances, I have no duties, but this is a mistake. Among the actions which I could do at this moment are some wrong ones; I might, for example, throw my muffin in my friend's face, or wantonly break the window of the cafe in which I am drinking tea with him. Since it is within my power to perform, at this very moment, some wrong actions, I must, at this very moment, have some duty incumbent upon me, namely, the duty of refraining from performing any of these wrong actions. And furthermore, a man of more ascetic temperament and sterner moral character than myself might well argue that, at this very moment, I was not doing my duty; that my money might be better employed in succouring the needy; my time in furthering the development of a noble cause; my mind in contemplating the benevolence of my Maker or the enormities of my sins.

For these reasons, it seems to me that, so far from right actions almost always being duties, right actions are hardly ever duties. What is my duty is to perform one of the number of alternative right actions which I could perform; in doing any one of them I do my duty, though I could equally well have done it in doing any other. The occasion when we can say of one particular action that it, and it alone, is a duty, occurs comparatively seldom.

Utilitarianism might, then, be defined as the theory which holds that an action is right if there is no action within the power of the agent which would produce more good than it, and that it is my duty to perform some right action or other. The circumstances in which there is only one right action within the power of the agent will fall under

[3] See W. D. Ross: *The Right and the Good*, pp. 3-4.

this principle as a special case, and, when this special case arises, that right action will also be a duty.

I will not bore my readers by citing any of the well-known objections to utilitarianism, but there is one particular difficulty in this theory which, for the purpose of this article, is of special interest. There are some actions which we think we have a duty to do, although they themselves produce no good consequences, because such actions would produce good consequences if they were generally practised. There are some actions which we think we have a duty to refrain from doing, even though they themselves produce no harmful consequences, because such actions would produce harmful consequences if the performance of them became the general rule. I think I have a duty to vote for that person whose party I think would govern the nation best, although I do not think that the addition of my vote to the total number of votes which are cast for him is going to make any difference to the result of the election, simply because I realise that, if all his other supporters were to do as I do, and fail to go to the polls, the man would not be elected. I refrain from walking on the grass of a well-kept park lawn, not because I think that my walking on the grass is going to damage the lawn to such an extent as to detract from anybody's pleasure in contemplating it, but because I realise that, if everybody else who walked in the park were to do likewise, the grass in the park would be spoilt. These two duties cannot be derived from the duty of setting a good example, or of refraining from setting a bad example, for I should still feel them incumbent upon me, even if no-one were to know that I had defaced my ballot paper, and even if the park was empty of everyone but me.

Such facts, if they are facts, have not been entirely neglected by Utilitarians. Hume, for example, may have had them in mind when he distinguished between justice and benevolence. Of the social virtues of benevolence and humanity he says: "And as the good, resulting from their benign influence is in itself complete and entire, it also excites the moral sentiment of approbation, without any reflection on farther consequences, and without any more enlarged views of the concurrence or imitation of the other members of society." [4] Whereas of justice he says:

---

[4] L. A. Selby-Bigge: *Hume's Enquiries*, second edition, 1902, p. 304.

"The case is not the same with the social virtues of justice and fidelity. They are highly useful, or indeed absolutely necessary to the well-being of mankind; but the benefit resulting from them is not the consequence of every individual single act; but arises from the whole scheme or system concurred in by the whole, or the greater part of the society." [5] Comparing the virtues of justice and benevolence, he says: "The happiness and prosperity of mankind, arising from the social virtue of benevolence and its subdivisions, may be compared to a wall, built by many hands, which still rises by each stone that is heaped upon it, and receives increase proportional to the diligence and care of each workman. The same happiness, raised by the social virtue of justice and its subdivisions, may be compared to the building of a vault, where each individual stone would of itself fall to the ground; nor is the whole fabric supported but by the mutual assistance and combination of its corresponding parts." [6]

Benevolent actions, if I have interpreted Hume rightly, themselves produce good consequences, and would produce good consequences whether anybody else performed benevolent actions or not. A just action, however, would not produce good consequences if it was the only instance of its kind. Just actions only produce good consequences so long as the performance of just actions is the rule rather than the exception. This is why one may often be bound to perform a just action which has consequences which are harmful. I must perform it, even when it itself has harmful consequences, because it is an action of a kind the general performance of which is necessary to society. This is why justice is "conventional" in a way in which benevolence is not. Justice is conventional in that the benefit to be derived from it depends upon its customary observance. No benefit will be obtained from my practice of justice unless my fellows practise it too, and the same is true of them. This is not to say that I make an explicit agreement with them that we shall all behave justly in order to gain the benefits of justice. Indeed, our obligation to be just could not be derived from any such agreement, because the obligation to keep agreements is itself a subdivision of justice. Both I and my neighbours are not just because we agree to be just, but because we each realise that the common practice of justice is in the interest of all of us.

[5] Loc. cit.
[6] Op. cit., p. 305.

However, it is not certain that Hume did hold the view which I have just attributed to him. This view may easily be confused with, and Hume himself, I am afraid, failed to distinguish it from, another rather similar view. There are some actions which, besides being of a sort which would produce good consequences if generally performed, are themselves necessary to the production of these good consequences. If two men are rowing a boat, the boat will progress only so long as they both row, and will fail to progress if either of them stop rowing. In this case, the actions of either oarsman are necessary if the good which consists in the progress of the boat is to be secured. Such actions, since they are necessary conditions of the production of a certain good, do themselves produce good consequences, and so they must clearly be distinguished from those actions which, though they are of a sort the general performance of which would produce good consequences, do not produce good consequences themselves. Moreover, the good which consists in the movement of the boat cannot be split into parts, and part attributed to the actions of one oarsman, and part to the actions of the other; the whole of this good must be produced, or none of it. Hence the good in question must be considered as being equally the consequence of the actions of either man, and it is the whole of this good which each man must take into account when he is considering whether or not he has a duty to row. Now it may have been Hume's view that justice is a duty, not because just actions are of a sort which would produce good consequences if generally practised, but because just actions are severally necessary if any good is to be produced by the general practice of justice.

There are arguments which might be used to try to show that Hume held the latter of the two views which I have just distinguished; which tend to show that Hume thought that we had a duty to be just because, if we were not just, the whole of the good consequent upon the general performance of justice would be lost; rather than that he thought that we should perform just actions because they were of a sort the general performance of which would produce good consequences, even when they themselves did not. In the first place, he sometimes speaks as if the performance of every just action is necessary if any just action is to produce good consequences. I must be just, even when it seems that the consequences of my being just are bad, because, if I am not just, the good which the general practice of justice brings about will be lost. In the second place, he thinks that, in a state of nature, it will be nobody's duty to be just, because if, in such a state, only one of us behaves justly, no good will result. Whereas what he should have said—and, perhaps, what he would have said—if he had held that a just action is made right by the fact that it is of a sort the general performance of which would produce good consequences, is, that it is our duty to be just, even in a state of nature. For it is still true, even in a state of nature, that the general performance of just actions would produce good consequences, even though individual just actions, performed in that state, do not produce good consequences; hence, it seems, we would have a duty to be just in a state of nature, even if, by being just, we produce consequences which are indifferent, or even bad.

The fact that Hume thought that we would not have a duty to be just in a state of nature, and the fact that he sometimes speaks as if the performance of every just action is necessary if any just action is to have good consequences, seems to indicate that Hume thought that we had a duty to perform just actions because they, together with other just actions, were severally necessary to the production of the good resultant upon the practice of justice. But there are some arguments which tend to show, either that he thought that we had a duty to practise just actions because they were of a sort the general performance of which would have good consequences, or that, if he did not actually hold this, his theory is as a result a worse one than I have supposed it to be.

Firstly, the view that we must be just in this particular case, so that the good consequent upon the practice of justice as a whole should be brought about, is unrealistic. It is simply false that the performance of every just action is necessary if the good produced by the practice of justice is to be secured. If this were true, the human race would have perished miserably many years ago. An occasional act of injustice here and there does not undermine the whole beneficial effect of the practice of justice, and, if such actions are performed in secret, they may sometimes not even produce any harmful effects at all.

Secondly, the view that we must be just, because just actions are severally necessary to the production of the good of justice, would make our duty to be just more rigid than we in fact believe it to be. Our normal view on the practice of justice in hard cases is this. We think that we should not turn aside from justice whenever it seems that an unjust action would produce some good, but, on the other hand, we do think that there are occasions on which unjust actions should be performed, because the good to be gained is considerable. But, if the whole of the good consequent upon the practice of justice were dependent upon the performance of just actions in every particular case, it is difficult to believe that the consequences of any individual unjust action, considered in itself, could ever be good enough to justify me in performing it. I must, therefore, apply rules of justice in all circumstances, however trivial, and however great the immediate good to be gained by neglecting them.

Thirdly, if Hume did hold the view that we must perform just actions because just actions are necessary if the general practice of justice is to have any value, then his theory is incapable of accounting for the difficulties with which utilitarianism is faced, and for which it was, in part, intended to account. This theory was, in part, intended to explain how we could have a duty to perform some actions the consequences of which were indifferent or positively bad, and it is one of the great merits of the view that we have a duty to perform actions because they are of a sort which would produce good consequences if generally practised, that it does enable us to explain how it is that we have a duty to perform some actions which, in themselves, have bad or indifferent consequences. But the theory that it is our duty to perform just actions because their performance is necessary for the good of justice to be realised does not, in fact, do this. It does not, as does the other theory, admit and account for the fact that we have a duty to perform some actions which do not themselves produce good consequences, for it does not recognise that there are such duties. All that can be said, if we adopt it, is that there are some actions, which seem to produce no good consequences, or even to produce bad consequences, when we take a narrow and restricted view. When we take a more enlarged view, and consider these actions along with other actions of the same sort, it will be seen that, in actual fact, they really do produce good consequences; they produce good consequences because they are one of a set of actions the several performance of which is necessary if a certain good is to be produced. This view, therefore, does not find a place in the utilitarian scheme of duties for our duty to perform actions which do not themselves have good consequences. It merely denies that we have any such duties, and tries to explain how the illusion that we have arises.

Utilitarians—as well as moral philosophers who have not been utili-tarians—have not always failed to notice the fact that we think actions are right if they are of a sort which would produce good consequences if generally practised, or are wrong if they are of a sort which would produce bad consequences if other people did the same. Mill, for ex-ample, remarked: "In the case of abstinences—indeed of things which people forbear to do from moral considerations, though the conse-quences in the particular case might be beneficial—it would be unworthy of an intelligent agent not to be consciously aware that the action is of a class which, if practised generally, would be generally injurious, and that this is the ground of the obligation to abstain from it." [7] But utili-tarians have not always realised that, in admitting that the performance of such actions is a duty, they are departing from, or, at least, modifying, utilitarianism as it is stated above. And that they are departing from, or modifying, utilitarianism, as it is usually thought of, is clear. For actions which are permissible, according to utilitarianism as I have defined it above, might well not be permissible, according to utilitarian-ism in this modified form. For it may very well be true of an action, both that there is no other action within the power of the agent that would produce better consequences than it, and that it is an instance of a class of actions which would produce harmful consequences if they were to be generally performed. In this case, I should, according to utilitarianism as it is normally thought of, be acting rightly if I per-formed it; whereas, according to this modified form of utilitarianism, I should be acting wrongly.

But the principle that I should perform actions, if they are of a sort which would produce good consequences if generally performed, and should refrain from performing actions which would produce bad con-sequences, if generally performed, is not free from difficulty.

In the first place, the principle is, as it stands, insufficiently precise. An action, it says, is right if it is of a sort which would produce good consequences, if generally practised, and wrong if it is of a sort which would produce harmful consequences, if generally practised. But no action is an instance of just one sort or class of actions; every action is an instance of many such sorts. It may well be that among the many classes of action of which a given action is an instance, there may be some classes which would have good consequences, if generally per-

[7] John Stuart Mill: *Utilitarianism*, Everyman Edition, pp. 17-18.

formed, some classes which would have bad consequences, if generally performed, and yet other classes, the general performance of which would be indifferent. When we say that the consequences, for good or for ill, of the class of actions of which a given action is a member should be taken into account when we are considering whether or not that action ought to be performed, about which of the many classes, of which the action in question is an instance, are we talking? Which of these classes should be considered, when we are wondering whether such an action is a right and proper one for us to do?

Some of the classes, of which it is a member, should not be considered by us because the consequences which they would have, if generally performed, are different from the consequences their sub-classes would have, if they were generally performed. Suppose, for example, that a red-headed man with one eye, a wart on his right cheek, and a mermaid tattooed on his left fore-arm, were to tell a lie on a Tuesday. It might be argued that it was quite permissible for him to have told this lie, because his action in telling the lie belongs to the class of actions performed on a Tuesday, and the consequences of the general performance of actions on a Tuesday is indifferent. But the class of actions performed on a Tuesday is not the sort of class which it is important to consider, when meditating upon the consequences of the general performance of certain classes of actions. For the class of actions performed on a Tuesday contains within itself a number of sub-classes: deceitful actions on a Tuesday, self-sacrificing actions on a Tuesday, revengeful actions on a Tuesday, and so on. The consequences of the general performance of actions in these sub-classes will differ both from one another and from the consequences of the general performance of that wider class which is the genus. Since this is the case, it would be unreasonable for us to consider the consequences of the general performance of actions on a Tuesday. For the consequences of the general practice of lying on a Tuesday are different from those of the general practice of actions of any sort on a Tuesday, and it is the consequences of the general performance of the more specific class of actions which it is important for us to consider.

It can be important for us to consider the consequences of the general performance of a certain class of actions only if that class contains within itself no sub-classes, the consequences of the general practice of which is either better or worse than the consequences of the general practice of actions belonging to it. It would be inaccurate to say that this class is of the wrong sort because it is too generic. For the class of actions performed between 3.00 p.m. and 3.01 p.m. on Tuesday is a good deal more specific than it is, and yet is of the wrong sort for precisely the same reason.

If, on the other hand—to revert to our original example—we were to consider, not the consequences of the general practice of lying, but the consequences of the general practice of lying by one-eyed, red-headed men, with warts on their right cheeks and mermaids tattooed on their left forearms, then the class of actions we were considering would be a wrong one, but for a different reason. The class of actions performed on Tuesday afternoon was a wrong one to consider, because it could be "relevantly specified"; that is to say, by the addition of characteristics such as "being the telling of a lie" I could obtain a more specific class of actions, the consequences of the general performance of which would be different from the consequences of the general performance of actions belonging to it. The class of actions, "lies told by one-eyed, red-headed men, with warts on their right cheeks, and mermaids tattooed on their left fore-arms," is a wrong one because it can be "irrelevantly generalised"; that is to say, by subtracting characteristics such as "being an action performed by a one-eyed man" I can obtain more general classes of actions, the consequences of the general performance of which do not differ from the consequences of the general performance of actions belonging to it.

In the second place, the principle seems to rule out as being wrong a number of actions which everybody normally thinks to be permissible, and would make obligatory as duties many actions which people do not normally consider to be such. The principle that I should perform actions, the general practice of which would be beneficial, is often used as an argument for pacifism, and with some plausibility. If everybody were to refrain from participating in wars, there would be no wars; hence it is my duty to refrain from participating in wars, whether any-body else co-operates with me or not. But the same principle can be used to justify actions which even a pacifist would condemn. If nobody were to lay violent hands upon the persons of his neighbours, or upon their property, everyone would live in peace with his fellow men—and what a desirable state of affairs this would be! But must the policeman for this reason refrain from forcibly apprehending the criminal, the judge from sending him to prison, and the gaoler from keeping him there? Similarly, the principle that I should refrain from performing actions which would be harmful if generally performed would make it obligatory for me to refrain from performing many actions which I have, no doubt, a duty not to do. But it would also make it obligatory for me to refrain from performing many actions which we would all regard as being permissible, if not positively as duties. It would make it my duty, for example, not to become a professional philosopher, because, in a world in which everybody became professional philosophers, it would be impossible to survive. The same principle would prohibit entry into almost any trade or profession, with the possible exception of that of agricultural labourer.

But in answering the first difficulty, the means of answering this second difficulty have already been provided. It is true, for example, that if we consider violent actions generally, then, if everybody refrained from violent actions, good consequences would result. But the class of violent actions is not the class which it is important to consider, when we are wondering whether an action is of a sort which would have good or bad consequences if generally performed. The class of violent actions is not the right class for us to consider because it can relevantly be made more specific. It contains within itself, as sub-classes, such species of violent actions as the violence of a parent towards a child, the violence of a policeman towards a criminal, the violence of a criminal towards a householder, the violence of one soldier to another, the violence of one small boy to another small boy. Since the consequences of the general practice of these sub-classes of violent action may be, and very probably are, different from the consequences of the universal practice of violent actions in general, then it is the consequences of the general practice of the species which we should consider, not of the genus. So, too, participation in wars is a class of actions which can be made relevantly more specific, if it is limited by the addition of suitable characteristics. It contains sub-classes, such as participation in wars on behalf of an aggressor, participation in wars on behalf of a country which is resisting aggression, participation in wars as a mercenary on behalf of a country of which one is not a citizen, participation in religious wars, participation in disciplinary wars on behalf of some international authority. Since the consequences of the general performance of these

species will differ from the consequences of the general performance of
the genus, then it is the species which should be considered, not the
genus. To take the third example, if everyone were to become university
lecturers, the consequences would, no doubt, be deplorable. But the
entering into the profession of university lecturer is a class of actions
which contains species such as that of becoming a university lecturer by
men who have no aptitude for medicine, no liking for the civil service,
and who have a capacity for acquiring and disseminating information
which would be unsuitable for school-children, but of not much use or
interest to ordinary adults. Becoming a university lecturer is a class of
actions which can be relevantly specified, and, since this is so, it is the
consequences of the general practice of the species which we should
consider, not the consequences of the general practice of the genus.

Actions are right if they are of a sort which would produce good
consequences, if generally practised. Now being right is a property of
the individual action. Being generally practised (or seldom, or always,
or never practised, as the case may be) is a property of the sort of action
this action is, or of the class of actions of which it is a member. But of
what is producing good consequences a property? When actions of this
sort are not generally practised, producing good consequences will, of
course, be a property of nothing. But when actions of this sort are generally practised, of what will producing good consequences be a property?
Not of the sort, because sorts or classes cannot produce good consequences, or fail to produce them, though instances of the sort or members of the class can. Producing good consequences must, then, be a
property of the individual actions. But if we say that every individual
action of the sort produces good consequences, then our principle does
not meet the difficulty which it was introduced to meet, namely, the
difficulty that there are actions which are right, although they do not
produce good consequences. Whereas if we say that only some of the
individual actions of the sort produce good consequences, we are faced
with this perplexing situation: the rightness of some instances of the
sort is derived from the good consequences produced by other instances
of the sort. We are faced, too, with this further difficulty. A utilitarian,
if he is to deserve the name at all, must try to derive the rightness of
actions in some way from the good ends which they serve. So it may be
objected that, if the general practice of a sort of action produces good

consequences, even when some actions of the sort produce no good consequences, or even bad consequences, would not even better consequences be produced if people were to refrain from performing those actions of the sort which did not produce good consequences, and performed only those that did? [8] But if this is the case, then it cannot be argued that the rightness of those actions which do not produce good consequences is dependent on the fact that in some way they serve a good end, for this, so far from being a fact, is, as the preceding argument has shown, simply not true.

The argument I have just stated does not, I think, show that the man who holds that our duty to perform a certain action may be founded upon the good consequences of the general performance of similar actions cannot properly be called a utilitarian, but it does serve to elicit an important property which such classes of action must have. Consider, for example, the class of actions "drinking cocoa for breakfast". It may well be that actions of this class would have good consequences, if generally performed, and it may even be that this class of actions cannot relevantly be made more specific, in the way in which I have explained. But even so, the fact, if it is a fact, that actions of this sort would produce good consequences, if they were to be generally performed, could not possibly be an adequate reason for thinking that either I, or anybody else, has a duty to drink cocoa for breakfast. If I have a duty to drink cocoa for breakfast at all, this duty is derived from the effects of drinking cocoa on my health and temper, *i.e.*, on the effects of the particular action to be performed, not upon the effects of the general performance of similar actions.

If this is so, then the mere fact that actions of a certain class would have good consequences if they were generally performed cannot be sufficient to make performance of such actions a duty, even when the class in question cannot relevantly be made more specific. Something more is necessary. Actions of the class in question must be so related to one another that, if they are not performed in the majority of cases, then they will not produce good consequences—or, at any rate, not such good consequences—in any. They must be related to one another in such a way that the good consequences produced by those of them which do produce good consequences are dependent upon a sufficient

---

[8] See D. G. C. Macnabb: *David Hume: His Theory of Knowledge and Morality*, p. 182.

number of those of them which do not have good consequences being performed. Mr. R. F. Harrod, in an excellent article on the subject,[9] has characterised such classes (in the way in which one would expect of an economist) thus: *"There are certain acts which when performed on n similar occasions have consequences more than n times as great as those resulting from one performance. And it is in this class of cases that obligations arise."* [10] By obligation, apparently, Mr. Harrod does not mean just any sort of obligation. He means our obligation to perform certain actions, although we could produce better consequences by not performing them.

The difference between the view just outlined and the other theory which Hume might have held is this. According to the other theory, the performance of any action was necessary if the others were to produce good consequences. Hence the good consequences produced by the general performance of the class of actions was equally dependent upon the performance of every member of the class. According to the view just outlined, not every member of the class of actions in question must be performed if the others are to continue to have any value. I may omit to perform any one (or any two, or any three) of those actions which themselves produce no good consequences, without detracting from the value of those which do. But if we were to neglect to perform all the actions in the class which themselves had no good consequences, then the good consequences produced by the others would be seriously affected. Hence our objection is answered. Not to perform any one of the actions which themselves produce no good consequences would not detract from the good produced by the general performance of actions of the class, provided that the others continued to be performed. But not to perform any at all would seriously diminish it, if not take it away altogether.

Hence we must perform certain actions, which produce no good consequences, or even harmful consequences themselves, because, if everybody took the liberty of infringing the rule demanding their performance in the same circumstances, its utility would be lost. But we do not think that such rules should be applied in all circumstances. We do not, it is true, think that we should fail to apply a rule, simply because one particular failure to apply it would produce no bad consequences, or

[9] R. F. Harrod: "Utilitarianism Revised," *Mind*, 1936. Reprinted by permission of the Editor.
[10] *Op. cit.*, p. 148.

even if application of the rule produced harmful consequences, provided that these consequences are not harmful beyond a certain point. But we do not think that such rules should be applied, however disastrous the consequences of applying them are. We think that, if the consequences of a certain application of a rule are disastrous, or even bad beyond a certain point, then the rule should be set aside in this particular case. In other words, when benevolence conflicts with justice, we do not, as Hume seemed to imply, think that justice should always override benevolence. In what circumstances, then, should justice prevail, and in what circumstances benevolence?

We should, I think, only apply a rule to a hard case if the gain which would result from failing to apply the rule in all cases as hard or harder exceeds the loss which would result from failure to apply the rule to those cases. To suppose that the utility of a rule must be destroyed, or even greatly diminished, by failure to apply it in certain restricted instances is a mistake. If we were only to fail to apply it to the hardest of hard cases, the rule might be neglected so rarely that its utility might be undiminished. It is only when we cease to apply the rule to cases less hard that the utility of the rule is impaired, and, even so, the gain from relieving the hard cases may be sufficient to counter-balance the loss of some of the benefit derived from the general application of the rule. If the gain from relieving the hard cases is only just sufficient to balance the loss of utility to the rule, then it is a matter of indifference whether we apply the rule or not. If the gain is insufficient to do this, then the rule should be applied. Mr. Harrod, in the article I have just mentioned, sums up the matter thus: "A lie is justified when the balance of pain or loss of pleasure is such that, if a lie was told in all circumstances when there was no less a balance of pain or loss of pleasure, the harm due to the total loss of confidence did not exceed the sum of harm due to truthfulness in every case." [11] It should be remembered that, though the gain due to failing to apply a rule to a case which is not very hard is, in respect of every individual failure to apply the rule, smaller than the gain resulting from failure to apply a rule to a case which is very hard, not very hard cases occur much more frequently than very hard cases, and, in this respect, the not very hard cases have the advantage. On the other hand, the fact that not very hard cases are frequent means that the loss of utility to the rule by failure to apply it to them will be

[11] *Op. cit.*, p. 149.

correspondingly greater than the loss of utility caused by failure to apply it to the very hard cases.

Readers will have noticed that this modified form of utilitarianism agrees with intuitionism in the form in which it is held by Sir David Ross in that, according to both him and it, we should not break certain rules simply because the consequences of breaking them are better than the consequences of keeping them. But it is, in one important respect, superior to Sir David Ross's theory. He thinks that we should pay our debts, keep our promises, honour our agreements, and tell the truth even in circumstances when we could produce more good by failing to do so. On the other hand, he quite properly does not hold the extreme view, that these rules should be observed, however great are the advantages of breaking them. In his own language, he thinks that we have a *prima facie* duty to bring about as much good as we can, as well as *prima facie* duties to keep our promises and tell the truth, and so on. When our *prima facie* duty to produce as much good as we can conflicts with our other duties, he thinks that sometimes it is a duty to perform the former *prima facie* duty, sometimes a duty to perform one of the others. But he is quite unable to provide us with any principle which will tell us when we should tell the truth, or keep the promise, and when we should tell the lie, or break the promise, in order to produce good consequences. He is quite sure that the principle by which we decide between these two conflicting rules is not what utilitarianism, as he understands it, says it is. According to the unmodified form of utilitarianism, we should tell the truth only so long as the consequences of truth-telling are better than the consequences of lying. If the consequences of truth-telling are just as good, or just as bad, as the consequences of lying, then it does not matter whether we tell the truth or not. If the consequences of lying are better than the consequences of telling the truth, then we should lie. Sir David Ross, on the other hand, thinks that we should not lie if the consequences of lying are only slightly better than the consequences of telling the truth, but that we should lie, if the consequences of lying are greatly better. But just how much better the consequences of lying must be than the consequences of telling the truth he is unable to tell us. But this modified form of utilitarianism can tell us, and it is, in this respect, if in no other, superior to Sir David Ross's view.

Utilitarianism, in its modified form, may also provide us with the solution to another of Sir David Ross's problems. What happens when, for example, my *prima facie* duty to tell the truth conflicts with my *prima facie* duty to keep my promises? Sir David Ross tells us that, when this happens, it is sometimes my duty to tell the truth, and sometimes my duty to keep my promise. But again, he is unable to provide us with any principle whereby we can decide between such conflicting *prima facie* duties. This, indeed, accords with his general view that, though rules can be given concerning what actions are *prima facie* duties, no rules can be given concerning what actions are duties.

Sir David Ross, though he thinks no principles can be given about duties, thinks that we do at least know enough about them to be able to reject the traditional utilitarian's way of solving the problem. We should not, he thinks, tell the lie and keep the promise, or tell the truth and break the promise, according to which of these two alternatives produces the most good. On this point he is probably right. But, it should be noticed, this is not the principle which the modified form of utilitarianism which we are discussing would recommend. We should not consider just the consequences of telling this lie and keeping this promise, or telling this truth and breaking this promise. We should consider what would be the consequences if everybody were to tell such lies in order to keep such promises or, what comes to the same thing, to break such promises in order to enunciate such truths. It may well be that, after reflection upon the general practice of such actions, we conclude that we should keep the promise and tell the lie, even though the consequences of breaking the promise and telling the truth would be better. It should be remembered, too, that the consequences of the general practice of keeping this sort of promise, or of telling this sort of truth, may differ from the consequences of the general practice of promise-keeping or truth-telling as genera.

So far, so good. But it may well be objected that we have no duty to perform an action simply because it is of a sort which would produce good consequences, if performed by everybody, or to refrain from performing it, because the general performance of it would be bad. Surely, it might be argued, we must be realistic about matters of duty. We should not base our conduct upon what would happen, if certain conditions, which may be unfulfilled, were realised. We should base our conduct upon what, after the fullest consideration possible in the time at our disposal, it seems most likely will happen. If, therefore, I can relieve a hard case by failing to apply a rule of justice, I should do so, even if the consequences of everybody doing the same would be bad, so long as I have reason to suppose that everybody will not do the same. Even if good consequences would be brought about by the general performance of a certain type of action, I have no duty to perform it, so long as I have good reason to believe that actions of that type will not, in fact, be generally performed. This, it might seem, is what Hobbes thought, and Hume—some of the time—because they both thought that we had not a duty to be just in a state of nature, i.e. in a state in which nobody else is just. Hume, though he thought that we had no duty to be just in a state of nature, thought that our duty to be benevolent was still incumbent upon us, for our duty to be benevolent, unlike our duty to be just, is in no way dependent upon the performance of benevolent actions by other people. Hence, in a state of nature, I have a duty to be benevolent to my fellows and to women[12] and domestic animals, though I have no duty to be just to them.

Mr. Harrod has an answer to this problem, which does not seem to me to be satisfactory. He says: "I believe that, where the practice is not general, a second refining process is required. Will the gain due to its application by all conscientious, i.e. moral, people *only* be sufficient to offset the loss which the crude utilitarian principle registers? It may be objected that there are no moral people. To meet this, for the word moral in the second refining principle, say people sufficiently moral to act disinterestedly in this kind of case." [13]

This answer, however, cannot be accepted. It is being objected that we do not have a duty to apply the principle where nobody else applies it, and Mr. Harrod replies that we have a duty to apply it if there are enough moral people to do likewise. But wherein lies their morality? In applying the principle? But then, they cannot be moral if the principle is not moral, and it is the morality of the principle which is being

[12] "In many nations the female sex are reduced to like slavery, and are rendered incapable of all property, in opposition to their lordly masters. But though the males, when united, have in all countries bodily force sufficient to maintain this severe tyranny, yet such are the insinuation, address and charms of their fair companions that women are commonly able to break the confederacy, and share with the other sex in all the rights and privileges of society." L. A. Selby-Bigge: *Hume's Enquiries,* p. 191.
[13] *Op. cit.,* p. 151.

called in question—and actually, by Mr. Harrod himself, set aside, in favour of the principle as doubly refined. And how many people are there moral enough to apply the principle in a state of nature? Surely, none at all, for a state of nature is defined as one in which there is nobody moral enough to apply the principle.

I think that Mr. Harrod, under the guise of defending the principle that the good or bad consequences of the general performance of a certain type of action should be considered, is really siding with its opponents. For I think that he really believes that it is important to know how many people there are sufficiently moral to apply the principle which I apply, because he thinks that it is important for me to know how likely it is that other people will apply the principle, before I can make up my mind whether I myself have a duty to apply it. But this is just what opponents of the principle think. They think that I have not a duty to be just rather than to relieve a hard case, even if the consequences which would result if everybody were to be unjust in similar cases would be bad, so long as I have reason to believe that other people will not be unjust in similar cases. They think that I have not a duty to be just in a state of nature, even though good consequences would result if everybody were to be just, because I have reason to believe that I shall be alone in my practice of justice.

To the man who objects that one may be unjust to relieve a hard case, even if such an action would have bad consequences if everybody else were to do the same, provided that I have reason to believe that nobody else will do the same, one is inclined to make the following answer. I am not in a better position to estimate what other people will do than they are to estimate what I will do and, if everybody were to relieve hard cases because they thought that it was unlikely that other people would do the same, bad consequences would result. We are inclined to say, if nobody were just in a state of nature, because they thought it unlikely that justice would also be practised by others, then we would never get out of a state of nature. If it be objected that we were never in a state of nature, it may be replied that we are all in a state of nature with regard to some things. Men may not be in a state of nature with regard to debt-paying, nor Englishmen with regard to queueing, but nations are in a state of nature with regard to international agreements, and housewives are, very likely, in a state of nature with regard to saving scrap, when they are told that, if everybody handed in their old dustbin lids, enough metal would be saved to build a battle-ship.

But, of course, in making these answers, we are not justifying the principle—though we are making it more plausible—for we are falling back on the very principle we are trying to justify. Nor is it possible to justify the principle. If it is true, then it must be accepted as true without reason, though this does not mean that it is irrational to accept it. In this respect it is like any fundamental moral principle, so the fact that it cannot be justified must not be held against it.

But the probability or otherwise of other people doing what I do does have a bearing on my duty to do an action (or to refrain from doing it) if it would have good (or bad) consequences if everybody else did the same. It is true that, if I only have good reason for thinking that other people will not do what I do, then my duty to be just in a hard case still applies. For other people's reasons for thinking that theirs will not be the general practice are as good as mine and, if everybody failed to apply a rule in a hard case merely because they had good reasons for thinking that others would not do the same, bad consequences would result. But if I had conclusive reasons for thinking that other people would not do the same, then it would be my duty to relieve the hard case. For only one person can have conclusive reasons for thinking that others will not relieve the hard cases he relieves, and, from one person's relieving hard cases, no disastrous consequences follow. Similarly, in a state of nature, if I only have good reasons for thinking that others will not apply the rules I apply, my duty to apply these rules remains. But if I have conclusive reasons for thinking that others will not apply the rules I apply, my duty to apply them ceases. For if everybody were to fail to apply these rules only in circumstances in which they knew that nobody else would do the same, no bad consequences would follow. If these two examples seem artificial, this is only because I have considered extreme cases. It is unlikely that I should know that nobody but I will fail to apply a rule of justice in a hard case, and it is unlikely that I should know that no-one but I will be just in a state bordering upon a state of nature. But I may sometimes know that the majority of people will not apply a rule to cases as hard as the case to which I fail to apply it, or know that the majority of people are too short-sighted and unrestrained to apply a rule of justice in cases where others do not. In such cases, supposing imitation by a minority of people only is not sufficient to produce any good (or bad) effects, my duty to apply the rule ceases. This, however, is not an exception to the principles already expounded, but a consequence of them. What I am saying, in other words, is that my knowledge of the behaviour of other people is a characteristic which relevantly specifies the class of actions the consequences of the general practice of which it is my duty to consider. I have a duty to perform a certain action, although believing that other people will not perform it, because, if everybody who believed that other people would not perform it were to do similar actions, good consequences would result. I have not a duty to perform an action, when knowing that other people will not do likewise because, if people performed similar actions only when they knew no-one else would do the same, no good consequences would follow.

My duty to perform actions of a sort which would have good consequences if they were generally practised will thus depend, in some measure, upon my ignorance of the behaviour of other people. I must not, for example, turn aside from applying a principle of justice in a hard case when I do not know that other people will not do the same, because I have every reason to believe that they will have much the same reasons for failing to apply a rule of justice to similar hard cases as I have for failing to apply it to this one, and because, if everybody were to do what I propose doing, disastrous consequences would follow. But, if I were omniscient about the behaviour of other people, then it would be my duty to do that action, which itself has good consequences. But this is not because the principle that we ought always to perform those actions which would have good consequences, if generally performed, and to refrain from performing those actions which would have bad consequences, if generally performed, is not applicable to people who have complete knowledge of the behaviour of others. It is because, to people who have complete knowledge of the behaviour of others, the two principles, that we should perform those actions which themselves have good consequences, and that we should perform those actions which are of a sort which would have good consequences, if practised generally, enjoin the same actions. If everybody having complete knowledge of the behaviour of other people were to perform those actions which themselves had good consequences, good consequences would result; whereas, if all people not having complete knowledge of the behaviour of other people were to perform those actions which themselves had good consequences, bad consequences would result. In the case of people having complete knowledge of the behaviour of others, the unmodified utilitarian principle falls under the modified principle as a special case, and an omniscient being would be justified in acting upon it, though beings like ourselves would not.[14] This does not mean, of course, that the two principles are identical. They would not be identical, even if they always enjoined identical actions, whereas they only do this in very special circumstances. Even when they enjoin identical actions, it is the modified utilitarian principle which is obligatory. The unmodified principle derives its obligatoriness from its accordance with the modified principle, and it is not obligatory in its own right.

It will not have escaped the reader, and it certainly did not escape Mr. Harrod, that there is some connection between the modified utilitarian principle and the Kantian categorical imperative. Now I do not think that the modified utilitarian principle can be deduced, as Kant thought moral principles could be deduced from the idea of law in general. The claim that moral principles can be deduced from the idea of law in general depends, I think, upon the claim that there is only one set of principles upon which, taken singly or together, it is possible for everybody to act, coupled with a definition of "law" according to which no principle upon which everybody cannot act can properly be said to be a law. It does not seem to me that the claim that there is only one set of principles upon which everybody can act is justified. A universe in which everybody acted morally is perfectly conceivable, but so is a universe in which everybody acted morally, with the exception that everybody committed suicide at the age of fifty. The fact that it is possible for everybody to commit suicide at the age of fifty (and, at the

---

[14] Cf. Butler: *Works, Gladstone's Edition*, vol. II, p. 190 n. "For instance: As we are not competent judges, what is upon the whole for the good of the world, there may be other immediate ends appointed us to pursue, besides that one of doing good, or producing happiness. Though the good of the creation be the only end of the Author of it, yet he may have laid us under particular obligations, which we may discern and feel ourselves under, quite distinct from a perception, that the observance or violation of them is for the happiness or misery of our fellow-creatures." Also C. D. Broad: *Five Types of Ethical Theory*, pp. 81-82.

same time, to be moral in other respects) does not seem to me to show that it is obligatory, or even permissible, to do this.

Nor do I think that imperfect duties can be derived from the impossibility of one's being able to will that everybody should fail to perform an imperfect duty. First of all it is not clear to me that this is impossible. If a man were sufficiently callous to murder his own wife, might he not be sufficiently callous, supposing he had the power, to will that other men should murder theirs? Besides, why cannot one will that everybody should fail to perform an (imperfect) duty? Not because of the moral repugnance such general negligence would cause us; Kant is supposed to be giving our inability to will that an action should be generally performed as a reason for thinking that it is wrong, and not *vice versa*. Are we unable to will general neglect of a duty, because such neglect would be contrary to our interest? Kant speaks as if I cannot will that people should not help others in distress, because, in that case, no one would help me when I am in distress. But, if the fact that an action has consequences which are detrimental to my interest is a bad reason for thinking that it is wrong, surely the fact that I cannot, from self interest, will its universal performance, is a worse one.

But the modified utilitarian principle, though it is not impossible for everybody to fail to act upon it, and though it is not impossible, though it may be immoral, for one to will that everybody should transgress it, does conform to some suggestions which may be found in the works of Kant. First of all, the unmodified utilitarian principle is self-defeating, whereas the modified principle is not. If everybody were to act upon the unmodified utilitarian principle, everybody would fail to apply rules of justice to certain hard cases, and bad consequences would result. But the purpose of the people who applied the unmodified utilitarian principle would be to produce good consequences, and so the general application of the rule they were practising would defeat the ends which determined them to adopt it.

Secondly, suppose that I apply the unmodified utilitarian principle to a certain case, knowing that, if other people apply the modified principle, I can produce good consequences by doing so. In this case, my conduct, though beneficial is, in a certain sense, inconsistent. It is not inconsistent in the sense that it is impossible for me to do what I do, nor in the sense that it is impossible for everybody to do what I do, nor in the sense that it is impossible for me to do what I do, while others do what they do. My principle is inconsistent with theirs in the sense that both of them could not be acted upon by everybody or, for that matter, by anybody. Since my own principle would be self-defeating if universally adopted, I do not regard it as fit for application by everybody, but take the liberty of allowing myself to make an exception to the ones that I do regard as suitable. Should it be argued, on behalf of a more nearly Kantian position, that my principle is really "Apply the unmodified utilitarian formula, so long as everybody else applies the modified formula," and that this principle cannot be acted upon by everybody, I reply that this argument rests upon a confusion. A judge is applying the principle "Condemn all murderers" just as much when he frees an innocent man as when he sentences a murderer. Similarly, the rest of the world, which is applying the modified utilitarian formula, may just as much be acting on the principle "Apply the unmodified utilitarian formula, so long as everybody else applies the modified formula" as am I, who apply the unmodified formula. What is impossible, is not that everybody should apply this principle, but that it should ever enjoin more than one person to apply the unmodified utilitarian formula.

The result is some reconciliation between the doctrine of Kant and the teleological ethical principles which he despised. An end, we must say, stands in much the same relation to the morality of principles as do the "facts" in relation to the truth of propositions, and we can no more decide what principles are and are not moral, by means of consistency alone, without reference to ends, than we can settle what propositions are true, by means of consistency alone, without reference to "facts." But though the fitness of any principle to be a moral principle cannot be decided without some reference to an end, the principle must be such that this end is harmoniously and coherently realised by its universal application and, if it can be successfully applied only by a given individual who relies upon the methods of others being more orthodox than his own, the principle is not one which deserves to be called "moral."

In other words, the unmodified utilitarian principle is not eligible to be part of a system of universal legislation, whereas the modified principle is, though it is not the only principle which is. In this respect the modified principle does, while the unmodified principle does not, conform to one of the conditions which any principle must fulfill if it is to be regarded as a principle on which we ought to act, and this condition it is one of Kant's great merits to have emphasised. No principle is fit to be a moral principle unless it is fit that it should be universally adopted and universally applied, though a principle may be unfit for universal adoption, even where universal adoption is logically possible. Our attitude to a principle cannot be a distinctively moral one unless we are prepared to accept, and sometimes to recommend, its universal application. The unmodified utilitarian principle conforms to neither of these two conditions. It is not fit for universal adoption, because the very grounds, namely, that it serves a good end, which recommend its application by one person, prohibit its application by everybody. And our attitude to it cannot be a moral one. For we can be prepared to apply it ourselves only so long as others do not, and hence we cannot possibly be prepared to recommend that it be adopted by others besides ourselves.

Justice as Fairness[1]

JOHN RAWLS

1. It might seem at first sight that the concepts of justice and fairness are the same, and that there is no reason to distinguish them, or to say that one is more fundamental than the other. I think that this impression is mistaken. In this paper I wish to show that the fundamental idea in the concept of justice is fairness; and I wish to offer an analysis of the concept of justice from this point of view. To bring out the force of this claim, and the analysis based upon it, I shall then argue that it is this aspect of justice for which utilitarianism, in its classical form, is unable to account, but which is expressed, even if misleadingly, by the idea of the social contract.

To start with I shall develop a particular conception of justice by stating and commenting upon two principles which specify it, and by considering the circumstances and conditions under which they may be thought to arise. The principles defining this conception, and the conception itself, are, of course, familiar. It may be possible, however, by using the notion of fairness as a framework, to assemble and to look at them in a new way. Before stating this conception, however, the following preliminary matters should be kept in mind.

Throughout I consider justice only as a virtue of social institutions, or what I shall call practices.[2] The principles of justice are regarded as

Reprinted from *The Philosophical Review*, vol. LXVII (1958), pp. 164-194, by permission of the author and the editors. The last paragraph of Section 3 has been extensively revised.

[1] An abbreviated version of this paper (less than one-half the length) was presented in a symposium with the same title at the American Philosophical Association, Eastern Division, December 28, 1957, and appeared in the *Journal of Philosophy*, LIV, 653-662.

[2] I use the word "practice" throughout as a sort of technical term meaning any form of activity specified by a system of rules which defines offices, roles, moves, penalties, defenses, and so on, and which gives the activity its structure. As examples one may think of games and rituals, trials and parliaments, markets and systems of property. I have attempted a partial anlysis of the notion of a practice in a paper "Two Concepts of Rules," *Philosophical Review*, LXIV (1955), 3-32.

formulating restrictions as to how practices may define positions and offices, and assign thereto powers and liabilities, rights and duties. Justice as a virtue of particular actions or of persons I do not take up at all. It is important to distinguish these various subjects of justice, since the meaning of the concept varies according to whether it is applied to practices, particular actions, or persons. These meanings are, indeed, connected, but they are not identical. I shall confine my discussion to the sense of justice as applied to practices, since this sense is the basic one. Once it is understood, the other senses should go quite easily.

Justice is to be understood in its customary sense as representing but *one* of the many virtues of social institutions, for these may be antiquated, inefficient, degrading, or any number of other things, without being unjust. Justice is not to be confused with an all inclusive vision of a good society; it is only one part of any such conception. It is important, for example, to distinguish that sense of equality which is an aspect of the concept of justice from that sense of equality which belongs to a more comprehensive social ideal. There may well be inequalities which one concedes are just, or at least not unjust, but which, nevertheless, one wishes, on other grounds, to do away with. I shall focus attention, then, on the usual sense of justice in which it is essentially the elimination of arbitrary distinctions and the establishment, within the structure of a practice, of a proper balance between competing claims.

Finally, there is no need to consider the principles discussed below as *the* principles of justice. For the moment it is sufficient that they are typical of a family of principles normally associated with the concept of justice. The way in which the principles of this family resemble one another, as shown by the background against which they may be thought to arise, will be made clear by the whole of the subsequent argument.

2. The conception of justice which I want to develop may be stated in the form of two principles as follows: first, each person participating in a practice, or affected by it, has an equal right to the most extensive liberty compatible with a like liberty for all; and second, inequalities are arbitrary unless it is reasonable to expect that they will work out for everyone's advantage, and provided the positions and offices to which they attach, or from which they may be gained, are open to all. These

principles express justice as a complex of three ideas: liberty, equality, and reward for services contributing to the common good.[3]

The term "person" is to be construed variously depending on the circumstances. On some occasions it will mean human individuals, but in others it may refer to nations, provinces, business firms, churches, teams, and so on. The principles of justice apply in all these instances, although there is a certain logical priority to the case of human individuals. As I shall use the term "person," it will be ambiguous in the manner indicated.

The first principle holds, of course, only if other things are equal: that is, while there must always be a justification for departing from the initial position of equal liberty (which is defined by the pattern of rights and duties, powers and liabilities, established by a practice), and the burden of proof is placed on him who would depart from it, nevertheless, there can be, and often there is, a justification for doing so. Now, that similar particular cases, as defined by a practice, should be treated similarly as they arise, is part of the very concept of a practice; it is involved in the notion of an activity in accordance with rules.[4] The first principle expresses an analogous conception, but as applied to the structure of practices themselves. It holds, for example, that there is a presumption against the distinctions and classifications made by legal systems and other practices to the extent that they infringe on the original and equal liberty of the persons participating in them. The second principle defines how this presumption may be rebutted.

It might be argued at this point that justice requires only an equal liberty. If, however, a greater liberty were possible for all without loss or conflict, then it would be irrational to settle on a lesser liberty. There is

[3] These principles are, of course, well-known in one form or another and appear in many analyses of justice even where the writers differ widely on other matters. Thus if the principle of equal liberty is commonly associated with Kant (see *The Philosophy of Law*, tr. by W. Hastie, Edinburgh, 1887, pp. 56 f.), it may be claimed that it can also be found in J. S. Mill's *On Liberty* and elsewhere, and in many other liberal writers. Recently H. L. A. Hart has argued for something like it in his paper "Are There Any Natural Rights?," *Philosophical Review*, LXIV (1955), 175-191. The injustice of inequalities which are not won in return for a contribution to the common advantage is, of course, widespread in political writings of all sorts. The conception of justice here discussed is distinctive, if at all, only in selecting these two principles in this form; but for another similar analysis, see the discussion by W. D. Lamont, *The Principles of Moral Judgment* (Oxford, 1946), ch. v.

[4] This point was made by Sidgwick, *Methods of Ethics*, 6th ed. (London, 1901), Bk. III, ch. v, sec. 1. It has recently been emphasized by Sir Isaiah Berlin in a symposium, "Equality," *Proceedings of the Aristotelian Society*, n.s. LVI (1955-56), 305 f.

no reason for circumscribing rights unless their exercise would be incompatible, or would render the practice defining them less effective. Therefore no serious distortion of the concept of justice is likely to follow from including within it the concept of the greatest equal liberty.

The second principle defines what sorts of inequalities are permissible; it specifies how the presumption laid down by the first principle may be put aside. Now by inequalities it is best to understand not *any* differences between offices and positions, but differences in the benefits and burdens attached to them either directly or indirectly, such as prestige and wealth, or liability to taxation and compulsory services. Players in a game do not protest against there being different positions, such as batter, pitcher, catcher, and the like, nor to there being various privileges and powers as specified by the rules; nor do the citizens of a country object to there being the different offices of government such as president, senator, governor, judge, and so on, each with their special rights and duties. It is not differences of this kind that are normally thought of as inequalities, but differences in the resulting distribution established by a practice, or made possible by it, of the things men strive to attain or avoid. Thus they may complain about the pattern of honors and rewards set up by a practice (e.g., the privileges and salaries of government officials) or they may object to the distribution of power and wealth which results from the various ways in which men avail themselves of the opportunities allowed by it (e.g., the concentration of wealth which may develop in a free price system allowing large entrepreneurial or speculative gains).

It should be noted that the second principle holds that an inequality is allowed only if there is reason to believe that the practice with the inequality, or resulting in it, will work for the advantage of *every* party engaging in it. Here it is important to stress that *every* party must gain from the inequality. Since the principle applies to practices, it implies that the representative man in every office or position defined by a practice, when he views it as a going concern, must find it reasonable to prefer his condition and prospects with the inequality to what they would be under the practice without it. The principle excludes, therefore, the justification of inequalities on the grounds that the disadvantages of those in one position are outweighed by the greater advantages of those in another position. This rather simple restriction is the main modification I wish to make in the utilitarian principle as usually understood. When coupled with the notion of a practice, it is a restriction of consequence,[5] and one which some utilitarians, e.g., Hume and Mill, have used in their discussions of justice without realizing apparently its significance, or at least without calling attention to it.[6] Why it is a significant modification of principle, changing one's conception of justice entirely, the whole of my argument will show.

Further, it is also necessary that the various offices to which special benefits or burdens attach are open to all. It may be, for example, to the common advantage, as just defined, to attach special benefits to certain offices. Perhaps by doing so the requisite talent can be attracted to them and encouraged to give its best efforts. But any offices having special benefits must be won in a fair competition in which contestants are judged on their merits. If some offices were not open, those excluded would normally be justified in feeling unjustly treated, even if they benefited from the greater efforts of those who were allowed to compete

[5] In the paper referred to above, footnote 2, I have tried to show the importance of taking practices as the proper subject of the utilitarian principle. The criticisms of so-called "restricted utilitarianism" by J. J. C. Smart, "Extreme and Restricted Utilitarianism," *Philosophical Quarterly*, VI (1956), 344-354, and by H. J. McCloskey, "An Examination of Restricted Utilitarianism," *Philosophical Review*, LXVI (1957), 466-485, do not affect my argument. These papers are concerned with the very general proposition, which is attributed (with what justice I shall not consider) to S. E. Toulmin and P. H. Nowell-Smith (and in the case of the latter paper, also, apparently, to me); namely, the proposition that particular moral actions are justified by appealing to moral rules, and moral rules in turn by reference to utility. But clearly I meant to defend no such view. My discussion of the concept of rules as maxims is an explicit rejection of it. What I did argue was that, in the *logically special* case of practices (although actually quite a common case) where the rules have special features and are not moral rules at all but legal rules or rules of games and the like (except, perhaps, in the case of promises), there is a peculiar force to the distinction between justifying particular actions and justifying the system of rules themselves. Even then I claimed only that restricting the utilitarian principle to practices as defined strengthened it. I did not argue for the position that this amendment alone is sufficient for a complete defense of utilitarianism as a general theory of morals. In this paper I take up the question as to how the utilitarian principle itself must be modified, but here, too, the subject of inquiry is not all of morality at once, but a limited topic, the concept of justice.

[6] It might seem as if J. S. Mill, in paragraph 36 of Chapter v of *Utilitarianism*, expressed the utilitarian principle in this modified form, but in the remaining two paragraphs of the chapter, and elsewhere, he would appear not to grasp the significance of the change. Hume often emphasizes that *every* man must benefit. For example, in discussing the utility of general rules, he holds that they are requisite to the "well-being of every individual"; from a stable system of property "every individual person must find himself a gainer in balancing the account. . . ." "Every member of society is sensible of this interest; everyone expresses this sense to his fellows along with the resolution he has taken of squaring his actions by it, on the conditions that others will do the same." *A Treatise of Human Nature*, Bk. III, Pt. II, Section II, paragraph 22.

for them. Now if one can assume that offices are open, it is necessary only to consider the design of practices themselves and how they jointly, as a system, work together. It will be a mistake to focus attention on the varying relative positions of particular persons, who may be known to us by their proper names, and to require that each such change, as a once for all transaction viewed in isolation, must be in itself just. It is the system of practices which is to be judged, and judged from a general point of view: unless one is prepared to criticize it from the standpoint of a representative man holding some particular office, one has no complaint against it.

3. Given these principles one might try to derive them from a priori principles of reason, or claim that they were known by intuition. These are familiar enough steps and, at least in the case of the first principle, might be made with some success. Usually, however, such arguments, made at this point, are unconvincing. They are not likely to lead to an understanding of the basis of the principles of justice, not at least as principles of justice. I wish, therefore, to look at the principle in a different way.

Imagine a society of persons amongst whom a certain system of practices is *already* well established. Now suppose that by and large they are mutually self-interested; their allegiance to their established practices is normally founded on the prospect of self-advantage. One need not assume that, in all senses of the term "person," the persons in this society are mutually self-interested. If the characterization as mutually self-interested applies when the line of division is the family, it may still be true that members of families are bound by ties of sentiment and affection and willingly acknowledge duties in contradiction to self-interest. Mutual self-interestedness in the relations between families, nations, churches, and the like, is commonly associated with intense loyalty and devotion on the part of individual members. Therefore, one can form a more realistic conception of this society if one thinks of it as consisting of mutually self-interested families, or some other association. Further, it is not necessary to suppose that these persons are mutually self-interested under all circumstances, but only in the usual situations in which they participate in their common practices.

Now suppose also that these persons are rational: they know their own interests more or less accurately; they are capable of tracing out the

likely consequences of adopting one practice rather than another; they
are capable of adhering to a course of action once they have decided
upon it; they can resist present temptations and the enticements of immediate gain; and the bare knowledge or perception of the difference
between their condition and that of others is not, within certain limits
and in itself, a source of great dissatisfaction. Only the last point adds
anything to the usual definition of rationality. This definition should
allow, I think, for the idea that a rational man would not be greatly
downcast from knowing, or seeing, that others are in a better position
than himself, unless he thought their being so was the result of injustice,
or the consequence of letting chance work itself out for no useful common purpose, and so on. So if these persons strike us as unpleasantly
egoistic, they are at least free in some degree from the fault of envy.[7]

Finally, assume that these persons have roughly similar needs and
interests, or needs and interests in various ways complementary, so that
fruitful cooperation amongst them is possible; and suppose that they
are sufficiently equal in power and ability to guarantee that in normal
circumstances none is able to dominate the others. This condition (as well
as the others) may seem excessively vague; but in view of the conception
of justice to which the argument leads, there seems no reason for making
it more exact here.

Since these persons are conceived as engaging in their common practices,
which are already established, there is no question of our supposing
them to come together to deliberate as to how they will set these practices
up for the first time. Yet we can imagine that from time to time they
discuss with one another whether any of them has a legitimate complaint against their established institutions. Such discussions are perfectly
natural in any normal society. Now suppose that they have settled on
doing this in the following way. They first try to arrive at the principles
by which complaints, and so practices themselves, are to be judged. Their
procedure for this is to let each person propose the principles upon which
he wishes his complaints to be tried with the understanding that, if
acknowledged, the complaints of others will be similarly tried, and that

[7] It is not possible to discuss here this addition to the usual conception of rationality.
If it seems peculiar, it may be worth remarking that it is analogous to the modification
of the utilitarian principle which the argument as a whole is designed to explain
and justify. In the same way that the satisfaction of interests, the representative claims
of which violate the principles of justice, is not a reason for having a practice (see sec.
7), unfounded envy, within limits, need not be taken into account.

no complaints will be heard at all until everyone is roughly of one mind as to how complaints are to be judged. They each understand further that the principles proposed and acknowledged on this occasion are binding on future occasions. Thus each will be wary of proposing a principle which would give him a peculiar advantage, in his present circumstances, supposing it to be accepted. Each person knows that he will be bound by it in future circumstances the peculiarities of which cannot be known, and which might well be such that the principle is then to his disadvantage. The idea is that everyone should be required to make *in advance* a firm commitment, which others also may reasonably be expected to make, and that no one be given the opportunity to tailor the canons of a legitimate complaint to fit his own special condition, and then to discard them when they no longer suit his purpose. Hence each person will propose principles of a general kind which will, to a large degree, gain their sense from the various applications to be made of them, the particular circumstances of which being as yet unknown. These principles will express the conditions in accordance with which each is the least unwilling to have his interests limited in the design of practices, given the competing interests of the others, on the supposition that the interests of others will be limited likewise. The restrictions which would so arise might be thought of as those a person would keep in mind if he were designing a practice in which his enemy were to assign him his place.

The two main parts of this conjectural account have a definite significance. The character and respective situations of the parties reflect the typical circumstances in which questions of justice arise. The procedure whereby principles are proposed and acknowledged represents constraints, analogous to those of having a morality, whereby rational and mutually self-interested persons are brought to act reasonably. Thus the first part reflects the fact that questions of justice arise when conflicting claims are made upon the design of a practice and where it is taken for granted that each person will insist, as far as possible, on what he considers his rights. It is typical of cases of justice to involve persons who are pressing on one another their claims, between which a fair balance or equilibrium must be found. On the other hand, as expressed by the second part, having a morality must at least imply the acknowledgment of principles as impartially applying to one's own conduct as well as to another's, and moreover principles which may constitute a constraint, or limitation, upon the pursuit of one's own interests. There are, of course, other aspects of having a morality: the acknowledgment of moral principles must show itself in accepting a reference to them as reasons for limiting one's claims, in acknowledging the burden of providing a special explanation, or excuse, when one acts contrary to them, or else in showing shame and remorse and a desire to make amends, and so on. It is sufficient to remark here that having a morality is analogous to having made a firm commitment in advance; for one must acknowledge the principles of morality even when to one's disadvantage.[8] A man whose moral judgments always coincided with his interests could be suspected of having no morality at all.

Thus the two parts of the foregoing account are intended to mirror the kinds of circumstances in which questions of justice arise and the constraints which having a morality would impose upon persons so situated. In this way one can see how the acceptance of the principles of justice might come about, for given all these conditions as described, it would be natural if the two principles of justice were to be acknowledged. Since there is no way for anyone to win special advantages for himself, each might consider it reasonable to acknowledge equality as an initial principle. There is, however, no reason why they should regard this position as final; for if there are inequalities which satisfy the second principle, the immediate gain which equality would allow can be considered as intelligently invested in view of its future return. If, as is quite likely, these inequalities work as incentives to draw out better efforts, the members of this society may look upon them as concessions to human nature: they, like us, may think that people ideally should want to serve one another. But as they are mutually self-interested, their acceptance of these inequalities is merely the acceptance of the relations in which they actually stand, and a recognition of the motives which lead them to engage in their common practices. *They* have no title to complain of one another. And so provided that the conditions of the principle are met, there is no reason why they should not allow such inequalities. Indeed, it would be short-sighted of them to do so, and could result, in

[8] The idea that accepting a principle as a moral principle implies that one generally acts on it, failing a special explanation, has been stressed by R. M. Hare, *The Language of Morals* (Oxford, 1952). His formulation of it needs to be modified, however, along the lines suggested by P. L. Gardiner, "On Assenting to a Moral Principle," *Proceedings of the Aristotelian Society*, n.s. LV (1955), 23-44. See also C. K. Grant, "Akrasia and the Criteria of Assent to Practical Principles," *Mind*, LXV (1956), 400-407, where the complexity of the criteria for assent is discussed.

most cases, only from their being dejected by the bare knowledge, or perception, that others are better situated. Each person will, however, insist on an advantage to himself, and so on a common advantage, for none is willing to sacrifice anything for the others.

These remarks are not offered as a rigorous proof that persons conceived and situated as the conjectural account supposes, and required to adopt the procedure described, would settle on the two principles of justice. For such a proof a more elaborate and formal argument would have to be given; there remain certain details to be filled in, and various alternatives to be ruled out. The argument should, however, be taken as a proof, or as a sketch of a proof; for the proposition I seek to establish is a necessary one, that is, it is intended as a theorem: namely, that when mutually self-interested and rational persons confront one another in typical circumstances of justice, and when they are required by a procedure expressing the constraints of having a morality to jointly acknowledge principles by which their claims on the design of their common practices are to be judged, they will settle on these two principles as restrictions governing the assignment of rights and duties, and thereby accept them as limiting their rights against one another. It is this theorem which accounts for these principles as principles of justice, and explains how they come to be associated with this moral concept. Moreover this theorem is analogous to those about human conduct in other branches of social thought. That is, a simplified situation is described in which rational persons pursuing certain ends and related to one another in a definite way, are required to act subject to certain limitations; then, given this situation, it is shown that they will act in a certain manner. Failure to so act would imply that one or more of the assumptions does not obtain. The foregoing account aims to establish, or to sketch, a theorem in this sense; the aim of the argument is to show the basis for saying that the principles of justice may be regarded as those principles which arise when the constraints of having a morality are imposed upon rational persons in typical circumstances of justice.

4. These ideas are, of course, connected with a familiar way of thinking about justice which goes back at least to the Greek Sophists, and which regards the acceptance of the principles of justice as a compromise between persons of roughly equal power who would enforce their will on each other if they could, but who, in view of the equality of forces

amongst them and for the sake of their own peace and security, acknowledge certain forms of conduct insofar as prudence seems to require.
Justice is thought of as a pact between rational egoists the stability of
which is dependent on a balance of power and a similarity of circumstances.[9] While the previous account is connected with this tradition, and
with its most recent variant, the theory of games,[10] it differs from it in
several important respects which, to forestall misinterpretations, I will
set out here.

First, I wish to use the previous conjectural account of the background
of justice as a way of analyzing the concept. I do not want, therefore, to
be interpreted as assuming a general theory of human motivation: when
I suppose that the parties are mutually self-interested, and are not willing
to have their (substantial) interests sacrificed to others, I am referring to
their conduct and motives as they are taken for granted in cases where
questions of justice ordinarily arise. Justice is the virtue of practices
where there are assumed to be competing interests and conflicting claims,
and where it is supposed that persons will press their rights on each
other. That persons are mutually self-interested in certain situations and
for certain purposes is what gives rise to the question of justice in
practices covering those circumstances. Amongst an association of saints,
if such a community could really exist, the disputes about justice could

[9] Perhaps the best known statement of this conception is that given by Glaucon
at the beginning of Book II of Plato's *Republic*. Presumably it was, in various forms,
a common view among the Sophists; but that Plato gives a fair representation of it is
doubtful. See K. R. Popper, *The Open Society and Its Enemies*, rev. ed. (Princeton,
1950), pp. 112-118. Certainly Plato usually attributes to it a quality of manic egoism
which one feels must be an exaggeration; on the other hand, see the Melian Debate in
Thucydides, *The Peloponnesian War*, Book V, ch. vii, although it is impossible to
say to what extent the views expressed there reveal any current philosophical opinion.
Also in this tradition are the remarks of Epicurus on justice in *Principal Doctrines*,
XXXI-XXXVIII. In modern times elements of the conception appear in a more
sophisticated form in Hobbes *The Leviathan* and in Hume *A Treatise of Human
Nature*, Book III, Pt. II, as well as in the writings of the school of natural law such
as Pufendorf's *De jure naturae et gentium*. Hobbes and Hume are especially in-
structive. For Hobbes's argument see Howard Warrender's *The Political Philosophy
of Hobbes* (Oxford, 1957). W. J. Baumol's *Welfare Economics and the Theory of the
State* (London, 1952), is valuable in showing the wide applicability of Hobbes's fundamental idea (interpreting his natural law as principles of prudence), although in this
book it is traced back only to Hume's *Treatise*.

[10] See J. von Neumann and O. Morgenstern, *The Theory of Games and Economic
Behavior*, 2nd ed. (Princeton, 1947). For a comprehensive and not too technical discussion of the developments since, see R. Duncan Luce and Howard Raiffa, *Games
and Decisions: Introduction and Critical Survey* (New York, 1957). Chs. vi and xiv
discuss the developments most obviously related to the analysis of justice.

hardly occur; for they would all work selflessly together for one end, the glory of God as defined by their common religion, and reference to this end would settle every question of right. The justice of practices does not come up until there are several different parties (whether we think of these as individuals, associations, or nations and so on, is irrelevant) who do press their claims on one another, and who do regard themselves as representatives of interests which deserve to be considered. Thus the previous account involves no general theory of human motivation. Its intent is simply to incorporate into the conception of justice the relations of men to one another which set the stage for questions of justice. It makes no difference how wide or general these relations are, as this matter does not bear on the analysis of the concept.

Again, in contrast to the various conceptions of the social contract, the several parties do not establish any particular society or practice; they do not covenant to obey a particular sovereign body or to accept a given constitution.[11] Nor do they, as in the theory of games (in certain respects a marvelously sophisticated development of this tradition), decide on individual strategies adjusted to their respective circumstances in the game. What the parties do is to *jointly* acknowledge certain *principles* of appraisal relating to their common *practices* either as already established or merely proposed. They accede to standards of judgment, not to a given practice; they do not make any specific agreement, or bargain, or adopt a particular strategy. The subject of their acknowledgment is, therefore, very general indeed; it is simply the acknowledgment of certain principles of judgment, fulfilling certain general conditions, to be used in criticizing the arrangement of their common affairs. The relations of mutual self-interest between the parties who are similarly circumstanced mirror the conditions under which questions of justice arise, and the procedure by which the principles of judgment are proposed and acknowledged reflects the constraints of having a morality. Each aspect, then, of the preceding hypothetical account serves the purpose of bringing out a feature of the notion of justice. One could, if one liked, view the principles of justice as the "solution" of this highest order "game" of adopting, subject to the procedure described, principles of argument for all coming particular "games" whose peculiarities one can in no way

---

[11] For a general survey see J. W. Gough, *The Social Contract*, 2nd ed. (Oxford, 1957), and Otto von Gierke, *The Development of Political Theory*, tr. by B. Freyd (London, 1939), Pt. II, ch. II.

foresee. But this comparison, while no doubt helpful, must not obscure the fact that this highest order "game" is of a special sort.[12] Its significance is that its various pieces represent aspects of the concept of justice.

Finally, I do not, of course, conceive the several parties as necessarily coming together to establish their common practices for the first time. Some institutions may, indeed, be set up *de novo;* but I have framed the preceding account so that it will apply when the full complement of social institutions already exists and represents the result of a long period of development. Nor is the account in any way fictitious. In any society where people reflect on their institutions they will have an idea of what principles of justice would be acknowledged under the conditions described, and there will be occasions when questions of justice are actually discussed in this way. Therefore if their practices do not accord with these principles, this will affect the quality of their social relations. For in this case there will be some recognized situations wherein the parties are mutually aware that one of them is being forced to accept

[12] The difficulty one gets into by a mechanical application of the theory of games to moral philosophy can be brought out by considering among several possible examples, R. B. Braithwaite's study, *Theory of Games as a Tool for the Moral Philosopher* (Cambridge, 1955). On the analysis there given, it turns out that the fair division of playing time between Matthew and Luke depends on their preferences, and these in turn are connected with the instruments they wish to play. Since Matthew has a threat advantage over Luke, arising purely from the fact that Matthew, the trumpeter, prefers both of them playing at once to neither of them playing, whereas Luke, the pianist, prefers silence to cacophony, Matthew is alloted 26 evenings of play to Luke's 17. If the situation were reversed, the threat advantage would be with Luke. See pp. 36 f. But now we have only to suppose that Matthew is a jazz enthusiast who plays the drums, and Luke a violinist who plays sonatas, in which case it will be fair, on this analysis, for Matthew to play whenever and as often as he likes, assuming, of course, as it is plausible to assume, that he does not care whether Luke plays or not. Certainly something has gone wrong. To each according to his threat advantage is hardly the principle of fairness. What is lacking is the concept of morality, and it must be brought into the conjectural account in some way or other. In the text this is done by the form of the procedure whereby principles are proposed and acknowledged (Section 3). If one starts directly with the particular case as known, and if one accepts as given and definitive the preferences and relative positions of the parties, whatever they are, it is impossible to give an analysis of the moral concept of fairness. Braithwaite's use of the theory of games, insofar as it is intended to analyze the concept of fairness, is, I think, mistaken. This is not, of course, to criticize in any way the theory of games as a mathematical theory, to which Braithwaite's book certainly contributes, nor as an analysis of how rational (and amoral) egoists might behave (and so as an analysis of how people sometimes actually do behave). But it is to say that if the theory of games is to be used to analyze moral concepts, its formal structure must be interpreted in a special and general manner as indicated in the text. Once we do this, though, we are in touch again with a much older tradition.

what the other would concede is unjust. The foregoing analysis may then be thought of as representing the actual quality of relations between persons as defined by practices accepted as just. In such practices the parties will acknowledge the principles on which it is constructed, and the general recognition of this fact shows itself in the absence of resent- ment and in the sense of being justly treated. Thus one common objection to the theory of the social contract, its apparently historical and fictitious character, is avoided.

5. That the principles of justice may be regarded as arising in the manner described illustrates an important fact about them. Not only does it bring out the idea that justice is a primitive moral notion in that it arises once the concept of morality is imposed on mutually self- interested agents similarly circumstanced, but it emphasizes that, funda- mental to justice, is the concept of fairness which relates to right dealing between persons who are cooperating with or competing against one another, as when one speaks of fair games, fair competition, and fair bargains. The question of fairness arises when free persons, who have no authority over one another, are engaging in a joint activity and amongst themselves settling or acknowledging the rules which define it and which determine the respective shares in its benefits and burdens. A practice will strike the parties as fair if none feels that, by participating in it, they or any of the others are taken advantage of, or forced to give in to claims which they do not regard as legitimate. This implies that each has a conception of legitimate claims which he thinks it reasonable for others as well as himself to acknowledge. If one thinks of the prin- ciples of justice as arising in the manner described, then they do define this sort of conception. A practice is just or fair, then, when it satisfies the principles which those who participate in it could propose to one another for mutual acceptance under the afore-mentioned circumstances. Persons engaged in a just, or fair, practice can face one another openly and support their respective positions, should they appear questionable, by reference to principles which it is reasonable to expect each to accept.

It is this notion of the possibility of mutual acknowledgment of principles by free persons who have no authority over one another which makes the concept of fairness fundamental to justice. Only if such ac- knowledgment is possible can there be true community between persons in their common practices; otherwise their relations will appear to them as founded to some extent on force. If, in ordinary speech, fairness applies more particularly to practices in which there is a choice whether to engage or not (e.g., in games, business competition), and justice to practices in which there is no choice (e.g., in slavery), the element of necessity does not render the conception of mutual acknowledgment inapplicable, although it may make it much more urgent to change unjust than unfair institutions. For one activity in which one can always engage is that of proposing and acknowledging principles to one another supposing each to be similarly circumstanced; and to judge practices by the principles so arrived at is to apply the standard of fairness to them.

Now if the participants in a practice accept its rules as fair, and so have no complaint to lodge against it, there arises a prima facie duty (and a corresponding prima facie right) of the parties to each other to act in accordance with the practice when it falls upon them to comply. When any number of persons engage in a practice, or conduct a joint undertaking according to rules, and thus restrict their liberty, those who have submitted to these restrictions when required have the right to a similar acquiescence on the part of those who have benefited by their submission. These conditions will obtain if a practice is correctly acknowledged to be fair, for in this case all who participate in it will benefit from it. The rights and duties so arising are special rights and duties in that they depend on previous actions voluntarily undertaken, in this case on the parties having engaged in a common practice and knowingly accepted its benefits.[13] It is not, however, an obligation which presupposes a deliberate performative act in the sense of a promise, or contract, and the like.[14] An unfortunate mistake of proponents of the idea of the social contract was to suppose that political obligation does require some such act, or at least to use language which suggests it. It is sufficient that one has knowingly participated in and accepted the benefits of a practice acknowledged to be fair. This prima facie obligation may, of

[13] For the definition of this prima facie duty, and the idea that it is a special duty, I am indebted to H. L. A. Hart. See his paper "Are There Any Natural Rights?," *Philosophical Review*, LXIV (1955), 185 f.

[14] The sense of "performative" here is to be derived from J. L. Austin's paper in the symposium, "Other Minds," *Proceedings of the Aristotelian Society*, Supplementary Volume (1946), pp. 170-174.

course, be overridden: it may happen, when it comes one's turn to follow a rule, that other considerations will justify not doing so. But one cannot, in general, be released from this obligation by denying the justice of the practice only when it falls on one to obey. If a person rejects a practice, he should, so far as possible, declare his intention in advance, and avoid participating in it or enjoying its benefits.

This duty I have called that of fair play, but it should be admitted that to refer to it in this way is, perhaps, to extend the ordinary notion of fairness. Usually acting unfairly is not so much the breaking of any particular rule, even if the infraction is difficult to detect (cheating), but taking advantage of loop-holes or ambiguities in rules, availing oneself of unexpected or special circumstances which make it impossible to enforce them, insisting that rules be enforced to one's advantage when they should be suspended, and more generally, acting contrary to the intention of a practice. It is for this reason that one speaks of the sense of fair play: acting fairly requires more than simply being able to follow rules; what is fair must often be felt, or perceived, one wants to say. It is not, however, an unnatural extension of the duty of fair play to have it include the obligation which participants who have knowingly accepted the benefits of their common practice owe to each other to act in accordance with it when their performance falls due; for it is usually considered unfair if someone accepts the benefits of a practice but refuses to do his part in maintaining it. Thus one might say of the tax-dodger that he violates the duty of fair play: he accepts the benefits of government but will not do his part in releasing resources to it; and members of labor unions often say that fellow workers who refuse to join are being unfair: they refer to them as "free riders," as persons who enjoy what are the supposed benefits of unionism, higher wages, shorter hours, job security, and the like, but who refuse to share in its burdens in the form of paying dues, and so on.

The duty of fair play stands beside other prima facie duties such as fidelity and gratitude as a basic moral notion; yet it is not to be confused with them.[15] These duties are all clearly distinct, as would be

---

[15] This, however, commonly happens. Hobbes, for example, when invoking the notion of a "tacit covenant," appeals not to the natural law that promises should be kept but to his fourth law of nature, that of gratitude. On Hobbes's shift from fidelity to gratitude, see Warrender, *op. cit.*, pp. 51-52, 233-237. While it is not a

obvious from their definitions. As with any moral duty, that of fair play implies a constraint on self-interest in particular cases; on occasion it enjoins conduct which a rational egoist strictly defined would not decide upon. So while justice does not require of anyone that he sacrifice his interests in that *general position* and procedure whereby the principles of justice are proposed and acknowledged, it may happen that in particular situations, arising in the context of engaging in a practice, the duty of fair play will often cross his interests in the sense that he will be required to forego particular advantages which the peculiarities of his circumstances might permit him to take. There is, of course, nothing surprising in this. It is simply the consequence of the firm commitment which the parties may be supposed to have made, or which they would make, in the general position, together with the fact that they have participated in and accepted the benefits of a practice which they regard as fair.

Now the acknowledgment of this constraint in particular cases, which is manifested in acting fairly or wishing to make amends, feeling ashamed, and the like, when one has evaded it, is one of the forms of conduct by which participants in a common practice exhibit their recognition of each other as persons with similar interests and capacities. In the same way that, failing a special explanation, the criterion for the recognition of suffering is helping one who suffers, acknowledging the duty of fair play is a necessary part of the criterion for recognizing another as a person with similar interests and feelings as oneself.[16] A person who never under any circumstances showed a wish to help others in pain would show, at the same time, that he did not recognize that they were

---

serious criticism of Hobbes, it would have improved his argument had he appealed to the duty of fair play. On his premises he is perfectly entitled to do so. Similarly Sidgwick thought that a principle of justice, such as every man ought to receive adequate requital for his labor, is like gratitude universalized. See *Methods of Ethics*, Bk. III, ch. v, Sec. 5. There is a gap in the stock of moral concepts used by philosophers into which the concept of the duty of fair play fits quite naturally.

[16] I am using the concept of criterion here in what I take to be Wittgenstein's sense. See *Philosophical Investigations* (Oxford, 1953); and Norman Malcolm's review, "Wittgenstein's *Philosophical Investigations*," *Philosophical Review*, LXIII (1954), 543-547. That the response of compassion, under appropriate circumstances, is part of the criterion for whether or not a person understands what "pain" means, is, I think, in the *Philosophical Investigations*. The view in the text is simply an extension of this idea. I cannot, however, attempt to justify it here. Similar thoughts are to be found, I think, in Max Scheler, *The Nature of Sympathy*, tr. by Peter Heath (New Haven, 1954). His way of writing is often so obscure that I cannot be certain.

in pain; nor could he have any feelings of affection or friendship for anyone; for having these feelings implies, failing special circumstances, that he comes to their aid when they are suffering. Recognition that another is a person in pain shows itself in sympathetic action; this primitive natural response of compassion is one of those responses upon which the various forms of moral conduct are built.

Similarly, the acceptance of the duty of fair play by participants in a common practice is a reflection in each person of the recognition of the aspirations and interests of the others to be realized by their joint activity. Failing a special explanation, their acceptance of it is a necessary part of the criterion for their recognizing one another as persons with similar interests and capacities, as the conception of their relations in the general position suppose them to be. Otherwise they would show no recognition of one another as persons with similar capacities and interests, and indeed, in some cases perhaps hypothetical, they would not recognize one another as persons at all, but as complicated objects involved in a complicated activity. To recognize another as a person one must respond to him and act towards him in certain ways; and these ways are intimately connected with the various prima facie duties. Acknowledging these duties in *some* degree, and so having the elements of morality, is not a matter of choice, or of intuiting moral qualities, or a matter of the expression of feeling or attitudes (the three interpretations between which philosophical opinion frequently oscillates); it is simply the possession of one of the forms of conduct in which the recognition of others as persons is manifested.

These remarks are unhappily obscure. Their main purpose here, however, is to forestall, together with the remarks in Section 4, the misinterpretation that on the view presented, the acceptance of justice and the acknowledgment of the duty of fair play depends in every day life solely on there being a *de facto* balance of forces between the parties. It would indeed be foolish to underestimate the importance of such a balance in securing justice; but it is not the only basis thereof. The recognition of one another as persons with similar interests and capacities engaged in a common practice must, failing a special explanation, show itself in the acceptance of the principles of justice and the acknowledgment of the duty of fair play.

The conception at which we have arrived, then, is that the principles of justice may be thought of as arising once the constraints of having a morality are imposed upon rational and mutually self-interested parties who are related and situated in a special way. A practice is just if it is in accordance with the principles which all who participate in it might reasonably be expected to propose or to acknowledge before one another when they are similarly circumstanced and required to make a firm commitment in advance without knowledge of what will be their peculiar condition, and thus when it meets standards which the parties could accept as fair should occasion arise for them to debate its merits. Regarding the participants themselves, once persons knowingly engage in a practice which they acknowledge to be fair and accept the benefits of doing so, they are bound by the duty of fair play to follow the rules when it comes their turn to do so, and this implies a limitation on their pursuit of self-interest in particular cases.

Now one consequence of this conception is that, where it applies, there is no moral value in the satisfaction of a claim incompatible with it. Such a claim violates the conditions of reciprocity and community amongst persons, and he who presses it, not being willing to acknowledge it when pressed by another, has no grounds for complaint when it is denied; whereas he against whom it is pressed can complain. As it cannot be mutually acknowledged it is a resort to coercion; granting the claim is possible only if one party can compel acceptance of what the other will not admit. But it makes no sense to concede claims the denial of which cannot be complained of in preference to claims the denial of which can be objected to. Thus in deciding on the justice of a practice it is not enough to ascertain that it answers to wants and interests in the fullest and most effective manner. For if any of these conflict with justice, they should not be counted, as their satisfaction is no reason at all for having a practice. It would be irrelevant to say, even if true, that it resulted in the greatest satisfaction of desire. In tallying up the merits of a practice one must toss out the satisfaction of interests the claims of which are incompatible with the principles of justice.

6. The discussion so far has been excessively abstract. While this is perhaps unavoidable, I should now like to bring out some of the features of the conception of justice as fairness by comparing it with the conception of justice in classical utilitarianism as represented by Bentham and Sidgwick, and its counterpart in welfare economics. This conception assimilates justice to benevolence and the latter in turn to the most

efficient design of institutions to promote the general welfare. Justice is a kind of efficiency.[17]

Now it is said occasionally that this form of utilitarianism puts no restrictions on what might be a just assignment of rights and duties in that there might be circumstances which, on utilitarian grounds, would justify institutions highly offensive to our ordinary sense of justice. But the classical utilitarian conception is not totally unprepared for this objection. Beginning with the notion that the general happiness can be represented by a social utility function consisting of a sum of individual utility functions with identical weights (this being the meaning of the maxim that each counts for one and no more than one),[18] it is commonly assumed that the utility functions of individuals are similar in all essential respects. Differences between individuals are ascribed to accidents of education and upbringing, and they should not be taken into account. This assumption, coupled with that of diminishing marginal utility, results in a prima facie case for equality, e.g., of equality in the distribution of income during any given period of time, laying aside indirect effects on the future. But even if utilitarianism is interpreted as

[17] While this assimilation is implicit in Bentham's and Sidgwick's moral theory, explicit statements of it as applied to justice are relatively rare. One clear instance in *The Principles of Morals and Legislation* occurs in ch. x, footnote 2 to section XL: ". . . justice, in the only sense in which it has a meaning, is an imaginary personage, feigned for the convenience of discourse, whose dictates are the dictates of utility, applied to certain particular cases. Justice, then, is nothing more than an imaginary instrument, employed to forward on certain occasions, and by certain means, the purposes of benevolence. The dictates of justice are nothing more than a part of the dictates of benevolence, which, on certain occasions, are applied to certain subjects. . . ." Likewise in *The Limits of Jurisprudence Defined*, ed. by C. W. Everett (New York, 1945), pp. 117 f., Bentham criticizes Grotius for denying that justice derives from utility; and in *The Theory of Legislation*, ed. by C. K. Ogden (London, 1931), p. 3, he says that he uses the words "just" and "unjust" along with other words "simply as collective terms including the ideas of certain pains or pleasures." That Sidgwick's conception of justice is similar to Bentham's is admittedly not evident from his discussion of justice in Book III, ch. v of *Methods of Ethics*. But it follows, I think, from the moral theory he accepts. Hence C. D. Broad's criticisms of Sidgwick in the matter of distributive justice in *Five Types of Ethical Theory* (London, 1930), pp. 249-253, do not rest on a misinterpretation.

[18] This maxim is attributed to Bentham by J. S. Mill in *Utilitarianism*, ch. v, paragraph 36. I have not found it in Bentham's writings, nor seen such a reference. Similarly James Bonar, *Philosophy and Political Economy* (London, 1893), p. 234 n. But it accords perfectly with Bentham's ideas. See the hitherto unpublished manuscript in David Baumgardt, *Bentham and the Ethics of Today* (Princeton, 1952), Appendix IV. For example, "the total value of the stock of pleasure belonging to the whole community is to be obtained by multiplying the number expressing the value of it as respecting any one person, by the number expressing the multitude of such individuals" (p. 556).

having such restrictions built into the utility function, and even if it is supposed that these restrictions have in practice much the same result as the application of the principles of justice (and appear, perhaps, to be ways of expressing these principles in the language of mathematics and psychology), the fundamental idea is very different from the conception of justice as fairness. For one thing, that the principles of justice should be accepted is interpreted as the contingent result of a higher order administrative decision. The form of this decision is regarded as being similar to that of an entrepreneur deciding how much to produce of this or that commodity in view of its marginal revenue, or to that of someone distributing goods to needy persons according to the relative urgency of their wants. The choice between practices is thought of as being made on the basis of the allocation of benefits and burdens to individuals (these being measured by the present capitalized value of their utility over the full period of the practice's existence), which results from the distribution of rights and duties established by a practice.

Moreover, the individuals receiving these benefits are not conceived as being related in any way: they represent so many different directions in which limited resources may be allocated. The value of assigning resources to one direction rather than another depends solely on the preferences and interests of individuals as individuals. The satisfaction of desire has its value irrespective of the moral relations between persons, say as members of a joint undertaking, and of the claims which, in the name of these interests, they are prepared to make on one another;[19]

---

[19] An idea essential to the classical utilitarian conception of justice. Bentham is firm in his statement of it: "It is only upon that principle [the principle of asceticism], and not from the principle of utility, that the most abominable pleasure which the vilest of malefactors ever reaped from his crime would be reprobated, if it stood alone. The case is, that it never does stand alone; but is necessarily followed by such a quantity of pain (or, what comes to the same thing, such a chance for a certain quantity of pain) that the pleasure in comparison of it, is as nothing: and this is the true and sole, but perfectly sufficient, reason for making it a ground for punishment" (*The Principles of Morals and Legislation*, ch. II, sec. iv. See also ch. x, sec. x, footnote 1). The same point is made in *The Limits of Jurisprudence Defined*, pp. 115 f. Although much recent welfare economics, as found in such important works as I. M. D. Little, *A Critique of Welfare Economics*, 2nd ed. (Oxford, 1957) and K. J. Arrow, *Social Choice and Individual Values* (New York, 1951), dispenses with the idea of cardinal utility, and uses instead the theory of ordinal utility as stated by J. R. Hicks, *Value and Capital*, 2nd ed. (Oxford, 1946), Pt. I, it assumes with utilitarianism that individual preferences have value as such, and so accepts the idea being criticized here. I hasten to add, however, that this is no objection to it as a means of analyzing economic policy, and for that purpose it may, indeed, be a necessary simplifying

and it is this value which is to be taken into account by the (ideal) legislator who is conceived as adjusting the rules of the system from the center so as to maximize the value of the social utility function. It is thought that the principles of justice will not be violated by a legal system so conceived provided these executive decisions are correctly made. In this fact the principles of justice are said to have their derivation and explanation; they simply express the most important general features of social institutions in which the administrative problem is solved in the best way. These principles have, indeed, a special urgency because, given the facts of human nature, so much depends on them; and this explains the peculiar quality of the moral feelings associated with justice.[20] This assimilation of justice to a higher order executive decision, certainly a striking conception, is central to classical utilitarianism; and it also brings out its profound individualism, in one sense of this ambiguous word. It regards persons as so many *separate* directions in which benefits and burdens may be assigned; and the value of the satisfaction or dissatisfaction of desire is not thought to depend in any way on the moral relations in which individuals stand, or on the kinds of claims which they are willing, in the pursuit of their interests, to press on each other.

7. Many social decisions are, of course, of an administrative nature. Certainly this is so when it is a matter of social utility in what one may call its ordinary sense: that is, when it is a question of the efficient design of social institutions for the use of common means to achieve common ends. In this case either the benefits and burdens may be assumed to be impartially distributed, or the question of distribution is misplaced, as in the instance of maintaining public order and security or national defense. But as an interpretation of the basis of the principles of justice, classical utilitarianism is mistaken. It *permits* one to argue, for example, that slavery is unjust on the grounds that the advantages to the slaveholder as slaveholder do not counterbalance the disadvantages to the

---

assumption. Nevertheless it is an assumption which cannot be made in so far as one is trying to analyze moral concepts, especially the concept of justice, as economists would, I think, agree. Justice is usually regarded as a separate and distinct part of any comprehensive criterion of economic policy. See, for example, Tibor Scitovsky, *Welfare and Competition* (London, 1952), pp. 59-69, and Little, *op. cit.*, ch. VII.

[20] See J. S. Mill's argument in *Utilitarianism,* ch. v. pars. 16-25.

slave and to society at large burdened by a comparatively inefficient system of labor. Now the conception of justice as fairness, when applied to the practice of slavery with its offices of slaveholder and slave, would not allow one to consider the advantages of the slaveholder in the first place. As that office is not in accordance with principles which could be mutually acknowledged, the gains accruing to the slaveholder, assuming them to exist, cannot be counted as in *any* way mitigating the injustice of the practice. The question whether these gains outweigh the disadvantages to the slave and to society cannot arise, since in considering the justice of slavery these gains have no weight at all which requires that they be overridden. Where the conception of justice as fairness applies, slavery is *always* unjust.

I am not, of course, suggesting the absurdity that the classical utilitarians approved of slavery. I am only rejecting a type of argument which their view allows them to use in support of their disapproval of it. The conception of justice as derivative from efficiency implies that judging the justice of a practice is always, in principle at least, a matter of weighing up advantages and disadvantages, each having an intrinsic value or disvalue as the satisfaction of interests, irrespective of whether or not these interests necessarily involve acquiescence in principles which could not be mutually acknowledged. Utilitarianism cannot account for the fact that slavery is always unjust, nor for the fact that it would be recognized as irrelevant in defeating the accusation of injustice for one person to say to another, engaged with him in a common practice and debating its merits, that nevertheless it allowed of the greatest satisfaction of desire. The charge of injustice cannot be rebutted in this way. If justice were derivative from a higher order executive efficiency, this would not be so.

But now, even if it is taken as established that, so far as the ordinary conception of justice goes, slavery is always unjust (that is, slavery by definition violates commonly recognized principles of justice), the classical utilitarian would surely reply that these principles, as other moral principles subordinate to that of utility, are only generally correct. It is simply for the most part true that slavery is less efficient than other institutions; and while common sense may define the concept of justice so that slavery is unjust, nevertheless, where slavery would lead to the greatest satisfaction of desire, it is not wrong. Indeed, it is then right, and for the very same reason that justice, as ordinarily understood, is usually right. If, as ordinarily understood, slavery is always unjust, to this extent the utilitarian conception of justice might be admitted to differ from that of common moral opinion. Still the utilitarian would want to hold that, as a matter of moral principle, his view is correct in giving no special weight to considerations of justice beyond that allowed for by the general presumption of effectiveness. And this, he claims, is as it should be. The every day opinion is morally in error, although, indeed, it is a useful error, since it protects rules of generally high utility.

The question, then, relates not simply to the analysis of the concept of justice as common sense defines it, but the analysis of it in the wider sense as to how much weight considerations of justice, as defined, are to have when laid against other kinds of moral considerations. Here again I wish to argue that reasons of justice have a *special* weight for which only the conception of justice as fairness can account. Moreover, it belongs to the concept of justice that they do have this special weight. While Mill recognized that this was so, he thought that it could be accounted for by the special urgency of the moral feelings which naturally support principles of such high utility. But it is a mistake to resort to the urgency of feeling; as with the appeal to intuition, it manifests a failure to pursue the question far enough. The special weight of considerations of justice can be explained from the conception of justice as fairness. It is only necessary to elaborate a bit what has already been said as follows.

If one examines the circumstances in which a certain tolerance of slavery is justified, or perhaps better, excused, it turns out that these are of a rather special sort. Perhaps slavery exists as an inheritance from the past and it proves necessary to dismantle it piece by piece; at times slavery may conceivably be an advance on previous institutions. Now while there may be some excuse for slavery in special conditions, it is never an excuse for it that it is sufficiently advantageous to the slave-holder to outweigh the disadvantages to the slave and to society. A person who argues in this way is not perhaps making a wildly irrelevant remark; but he is guilty of a moral fallacy. There is disorder in his conception of the ranking of moral principles. For the slaveholder, by his own admission, has no moral title to the advantages which he receives as a slaveholder. He is no more prepared than the slave to acknowledge the principle upon which is founded the respective positions in which they both stand. Since slavery does not accord with principles which they could mutually acknowledge, they each may be supposed to agree that it is unjust: it grants claims which it ought not to grant and in doing so denies claims which it ought not to deny. Amongst persons in a general position who are debating the form of their common practices, it cannot, therefore, be offered as a reason for a practice that, in conceding these very claims that ought to be denied, it nevertheless meets existing interests more effectively. By their very nature the satisfaction of these claims is without weight and cannot enter into any tabulation of advantages and disadvantages.

Furthermore, it follows from the concept of morality that, to the extent that the slaveholder recognizes his position vis-a-vis the slave to be unjust, he would not choose to press his claims. His not wanting to receive his special advantages is one of the ways in which he shows that he thinks slavery is unjust. It would be fallacious for the legislator to suppose, then, that it is a ground for having a practice that it brings advantages greater than disadvantages, if those for whom the practice is designed, and to whom the advantages flow, acknowledge that they have no moral title to them and do not wish to receive them.

For these reasons the principles of justice have a special weight; and with respect to the principle of the greatest satisfaction of desire, as cited in the general position amongst those discussing the merits of their common practices, the principles of justice have an absolute weight. In this sense they are not contingent; and this is why their force is greater than can be accounted for by the general presumption (assuming that there is one) of the effectiveness, in the utilitarian sense, of practices which in fact satisfy them.

If one wants to continue using the concepts of classical utilitarianism, one will have to say, to meet this criticism, that at least the individual or social utility functions must be so defined that no value is given to the satisfaction of interests the representative claims of which violate the principles of justice. In this way it is no doubt possible to include these principles within the form of the utilitarian conception; but to do so is, of course, to change its inspiration altogether as a moral conception. For it is to incorporate within it principles which cannot be understood on the basis of a higher order executive decision aiming at the greatest satisfaction of desire.

It is worth remarking, perhaps, that this criticism of utilitarianism does not depend on whether or not the two assumptions, that of individuals having similar utility functions and that of diminishing marginal utility, are interpreted as psychological propositions to be supported or refuted by experience, or as moral and political principles expressed in a somewhat technical language. There are, certainly, several advantages in taking them in the latter fashion.[21] For one thing, one might say that this is what Bentham and others really meant by them, at least as shown by how they were used in arguments for social reform. More importantly, one could hold that the best way to defend the classical utilitarian view is to interpret these assumptions as moral and political principles. It is doubtful whether, taken as psychological propositions, they are true of men in general as we know them under normal conditions. On the other hand, utilitarians would not have wanted to propose them merely as practical working principles of legislation, or as expedient maxims to guide reform, given the egalitarian sentiments of modern society.[22] When pressed they might well have invoked the idea of a more or less equal capacity of men in relevant respects if given an equal chance in a just society. But if the argument above regarding slavery is correct, then granting these assumptions as moral and political principles makes no difference. To view individuals as equally fruitful lines for the allocation of benefits, even as a matter of moral principle, still leaves the mistaken notion that the satisfaction of desire has value in itself irrespective of the relations between persons as members of a common practice, and irrespective of the claims upon one another which the satisfaction of interests represents. To see the error of this idea one must give up the conception of justice as an executive decision altogether and refer to the notion of justice as fairness: that participants in a common practice be regarded as having an original and equal liberty and that their common practices be considered unjust unless they accord with principles which persons so circumstanced and related could freely acknowledge before one another, and so could accept as fair. Once the

---

[21] See D. G. Ritchie, *Natural Rights* (London, 1894), pp. 95 ff., 249 ff. Lionel Robbins has insisted on this point on several occasions. See *An Essay on the Nature and Significance of Economic Science*, 2nd ed. (London, 1935), pp. 134-43, "Interpersonal Comparisons of Utility: A Comment," *Economic Journal*, XLVIII (1938), 635-41, and more recently, "Robertson on Utility and Scope," *Economica*, n.s. XX (1953), 108 f.

[22] As Sir Henry Maine suggested Bentham may have regarded them. See *The Early History of Institutions* (London, 1875), pp. 398 ff.

emphasis is put upon the concept of the mutual recognition of principles by participants in a common practice the rules of which are to
define their several relations and give form to their claims on one another, then it is clear that the granting of a claim the principle of which
could not be acknowledged by each in the general position (that is, in
the position in which the parties propose and acknowledge principles
before one another) is not a reason for adopting a practice. Viewed in
this way, the background of the claim is seen to exclude it from consideration; that it can represent a value in itself arises from the conception of individuals as separate lines for the assignment of benefits, as
isolated persons who stand as claimants on an administrative or benevolent largesse. Occasionally persons do so stand to one another; but this
is not the general case, nor, more importantly, is it the case when it is a
matter of the justice of practices themselves in which participants stand
in various relations to be appraised in accordance with standards which
they may be expected to acknowledge before one another. Thus however
mistaken the notion of the social contract may be as history, and however far it may overreach itself as a general theory of social and political
obligation, it does express, suitably interpreted, an essential part of the
concept of justice.[23]

8. By way of conclusion I should like to make two remarks: first, the
original modification of the utilitarian principle (that it require of
practices that the offices and positions defined by them be equal unless
it is reasonable to suppose that the representative man in *every* office
would find the inequality to his advantage), slight as it may appear at
first sight, actually has a different conception of justice standing behind
it. I have tried to show how this is so by developing the concept of
justice as fairness and by indicating how this notion involves the mutual
acceptance, from a general position, of the principles on which a practice
is founded, and how this in turn requires the exclusion from consideration of claims violating the principles of justice. Thus the slight altera-

---

[23] Thus Kant was not far wrong when he interpreted the original contract merely
as an "Idea of Reason"; yet he still thought of it as a *general* criterion of right and
as providing a general theory of political obligation. See the second part of the
essay, "On the Saying 'That may be right in theory but has no value in practice'"
(1793), in *Kant's Principles of Politics*, tr. by W. Hastie (Edinburgh, 1891). I have
drawn on the contractarian tradition not for a general theory of political obligation
but to clarify the concept of justice.

tion of principle reveals another family of notions, another way of looking at the concept of justice.

Second, I should like to remark also that I have been dealing with the *concept* of justice. I have tried to set out the kinds of principles upon which judgments concerning the justice of practices may be said to stand. The analysis will be successful to the degree that it expresses the principles involved in these judgments when made by competent persons upon deliberation and reflection.[24] Now every people may be supposed to have the concept of justice, since in the life of every society there must be at least some relations in which the parties consider themselves to be circumstanced and related as the concept of justice as fairness requires. Societies will differ from one another not in having or in failing to have this notion but in the range of cases to which they apply it and in the emphasis which they give to it as compared with other moral concepts.

A firm grasp of the concept of justice itself is necessary if these variations, and the reasons for them, are to be understood. No study of the development of moral ideas and of the differences between them is more sound than the analysis of the fundamental moral concepts upon which it must depend. I have tried, therefore, to give an analysis of the concept of justice which should apply generally, however large a part the concept may have in a given morality, and which can be used in explaining the course of men's thoughts about justice and its relations to other moral concepts. How it is to be used for this purpose is a large topic which I cannot, of course, take up here. I mention it only to emphasize that I have been dealing with the concept of justice itself and to indicate what use I consider such an analysis to have.

[24] For a further discussion of the idea expressed here, see my paper, "Outline of a Decision Procedure for Ethics," in the *Philosophical Review*, LX (1951), 177-197. For an analysis, similar in many respects but using the notion of the ideal observer instead of that of the considered judgment of a competent person, see Roderick Firth, "Ethical Absolutism and the Ideal Observer," *Philosophy and Phenomenological Research*, XII (1952), 317-345. While the similarities between these two discussions are more important than the differences, an analysis based on the notion of a considered judgment of a competent person, as it is based on a kind of judgment, may prove more helpful in understanding the features of moral judgment than an analysis based on the notion of an ideal observer, although this remains to be shown. A man who rejects the conditions imposed on a considered judgment of a competent person could no longer profess to *judge* at all. This seems more fundamental than his rejecting the conditions of observation, for these do not seem to apply, in an ordinary sense, to making a moral judgment.

Part Three

Justice

and the

Liberal Tradition

Equality and Equal Rights

RICHARD WOLLHEIM

I

The principle of Equality is an essential ingredient of the most enduring and articulate political tradition to come out of European culture: that of Liberalism. "Liberalism," as one of its finest historians has written, "regarded as a universal and widespread historical consciousness, implies not only the feeling of liberty but the idea of equality." [1] But like so much of that tradition, this principle has become so incrusted, so over-grown with particular interpretations, all comprehensible enough in the light of the particular historical conditions that occasioned them but, from an abstract point of view, partial and arbitrary, that it is difficult to see it clearly, as it is. Yet if we are to subscribe to it, or to reject it, or indeed to adopt any attitude towards it—as surely we all must—it is necessary to be clear about certain challenging questions that arise in connexion with it: what it means, how it can be justified, and in what relations it stands to the other principles with which it is ordinarily associated.

It would seem that in the course of history two quite distinct political principles have been advanced of which both can make a good claim to be regarded as the principle of Equality. It is not easy to bring out the differences between them, or indeed to express the principles themselves, by means of any general formulation. Accordingly I shall consider the principles through the medium of particular applications of them. For the sake of illustration I shall take the sphere of Property—a sphere

From the *Proceedings of the Aristotelian Society*, vol. 56 (1955-56), where it appeared with Professor Berlin's essay, which is also reprinted here. By permission of the author and of the Aristotelian Society.

[1] Guido de Ruggiero, *The History of European Liberalism*, trans. R. G. Collingwood (London, 1927), p. 51.

in which much has been heard of them. The two principles are there exemplified by the two following theses:

1. Every man has a right to equal property.
2. Every man has an equal right to property. (By "right" here, I mean of course "moral right": an equivalent formulation of these two theses could be constructed for "right" in the sense of "positive right" by substituting for "has" "ought to have".)

Now, I think that there are two striking differences between these two theses, and so by implication between the two principles on which they are based. Let us examine these in turn:

A.—According to the first thesis, everyone has a right to equal property: from which it follows that everyone has a right to property.[2] According to the second thesis, everyone has an equal right to property: from which nothing follows about anyone having any right to property. All that does follow is that if anyone has a right to property, no-one has either a greater or less right than he. The difference between these two claims is considerable, and this of course is magnified when we turn from the particular thesis to the general principles that lie behind them. For if these two principles are entirely general (as I take it they are), then that from which the first thesis is derived asserts that everyone has a right in all matters, in all respects: whereas the principle from which the second thesis is derived makes no assertion about the existence of anyone's rights in any matter of any respect.

B.—If the first thesis were adopted as a principle of political action, the resultant society would clearly be an egalitarian society: a society, that is to say, in which all commodities were distributed in equal quantities between the various members. It is clear, however, that the second thesis could be genuinely embraced and acted upon, and the society thereby brought into existence be far from egalitarian. For a supporter of this thesis might maintain that everyone has an equal right to property in that everyone has a right to the property he has worked to obtain, or everyone has a right to the property he can make use of, or everyone has a right to the property appropriate to his needs. Of course someone who maintained the principle in this way might be suspected of disingenuousness; and indeed might be disingenuous. But, then, he might not be. And if he wasn't, if that is to say he genuinely did

---

[2] This includes, of course, the limiting case of everyone having a right to zero quantity of property.

believe that people did have rights of these kinds and everyone had them equally, then surely we should have to allow that he did really subscribe to the principle that everyone has equal rights to property. Yet it is undeniable that this principle as held by him would lead directly to a society which not only contained but actively encouraged very considerable quantitative differences in the distribution of commodities between its members.

This latter point comes out even more clearly if we consider for a moment more "extremist" theories that might be, and indeed have been, held about the right to property. Someone, for instance, might hold that this right depends upon one's physical strength, or the purity of one's blood, or the colour of one's skin. Now as a fact—as a sad fact it might be said—not everyone possesses equally the characteristics on which this right depends: some people have whiter skins than others, some purer blood, some are of greater physical strength than their fellowmen. Accordingly any society that recognized this right would not be egalitarian: but because it respected it equally in all men, it could make a claim to have realized the principle of Equality. To put the matter in its most general form, any society, it seems, could make a claim to respect everyone's equal right to property provided that the variation in the amount of property possessed by the various members of that society could be correlated with a variation in some other general characteristic possessed by them—for this characteristic could always be cited as being that on which the right to property depends.

Now this is on the face of it a paradoxical situation and might well seem to many something much worse. For there can, I think, be no doubt but that it is the thesis of equal rights to property, not that of rights to equal property, or, more generally, the principle from which the former not the latter thesis is derived—what we might call the Principle of Proportional, as opposed to that of Quantitive, Equality —that belongs so integrally to the tradition of Liberalism. And if this is so, it seems highly unsatisfactory, to say the least of it, that this principle can be used to condone, indeed to encourage social arrangements that not merely are inegalitarian but by any reasonable standards are grossly inequitable. Surely, it will be argued, the principle of Equality is being travestied when it is quoted in justification of policies of, say, religious or racial discrimination. There must be some error or weakness in its formulation that permits such abuse of it. Accordingly, if the principle is still to fulfill its role as one of the main directives of liberal political policy, some effort is called for in the direction of greater rigour or clarity in its expression.

Such an objection, though sympathetic, is, I think, quite misconceived. For surely in all the cases of inequitable societies that claim to respect everyone's equal right to property, what is wrong with the claim is not a false interpretation of what it is for everyone to possess an equal right but a false view of what right it is that anyone possesses. The inference from, say, "A possesses the right to the property appropriate to the colour of his skin" to "Everyone possesses the right to the property appropriate to the colour of his skin" is perfectly unobjectionable: what is objectionable is the acceptance of the premiss "A possesses the right to the property appropriate to the colour of his skin." For it is not true that A possesses such a right; for there is no such right.

The only reason that I can see for denying that what seem like cases of equal distribution of "false" rights are ever really cases of equal distribution, is the view that no-one is ever really mistaken about what rights people possess. Everyone knows quite well what rights people possess—on this view—but some try to conceal this fact because they are neither prepared to deny the principle of equal distribution of rights nor prepared to accept the practical consequences of distributing equally such rights as there are; consequently they accord to some one right and to others another right and try to gloss this over by inventing a basis for their discrimination. Such a view seems to me totally unplausible. People can be hypocrites, but some I am sure aren't. Possibly one reason for thinking that more are than actually are lies in an ambiguity in the language of the attribution of rights. For someone might say "A has a right to the property he has worked for" and say this not just to specify the amount of property A has a right to, i.e., all that he has worked for, but to indicate the reason for this right or the characteristic on which it depends, i.e., that the property has been worked for. In such cases it is correct to infer from what he says that if he believes in the equal right to property he would admit that everyone else has a right to the property he has worked for. However, someone might say, "A has the right to the property that he has worked for" and say this only to specify the amount of property A has a right to, and wish to leave open the question of the reason for this right, the characteristic upon which it depends. But by assimilation of this case to the first, he might be taken to concede that everyone has the right to the property he has worked for, and accordingly when he explicitly denies this right to someone on account of the colour of his skin, be thought to have thereby forsaken the principle of equal rights to property. However, once we appreciate the true force (or true weakness) of his original attribution of A's right, we can see clearly that this is not so: and so *a fortiori* can see how little there is in the view that the equal distribution of "false" rights is always disingenuous.

But it might now be urged: Granted that someone does not violate the principle of equal rights merely by extending to all the right he has falsely attributed to one, does he not violate it by the original false attribution—for can one be said to accord everyone equal rights when one accords no-one his right? Here we seem to be on familiar ground. For the question as it stands is of the same form as others that occur over and over again in moral philosophy: Can a man be said to have done his duty when he has done only what he erroneously thought to be his duty? Can a man be said to have done to others what others ought to do to him when he has done to others what he believes others ought to do to him and his beliefs are false?

And surely the answer in all cases is No. For if, say, a man has done what he erroneously believes to be his duty, then it is false that what he has done is his duty, therefore what he has done is not his duty, therefore he has not done his duty. What is mysterious is why such questions should ever have caused any real perplexity, and why philosophers should have resorted to such unlikely expedients as "objective duty" and "subjective duty," "objectively right" and "subjectively right." Consider the question—Has a man told the truth when he has told what he believes to be the truth?—would any philosopher think that here was a reason for differentiating between the "objectively true" and the "subjectively true"?

Yet in philosophy there is never smoke without flame. I suggest that what lies behind the difficulty that philosophers have experienced in answering these simple questions is the doubt whether these are the proper questions to ask. And this in turn depends on the problem of how we are to interpret such principles as that of doing one's duty, or that of doing to others what others ought to do to one, or that of according to all equal rights. For we could see these principles as what might be called Rules of Life, that is to say, rules that we feel people should consult before they decide how to act. In that case the relevant question would be, for example, "Can a man claim to have done his duty when he has done what he erroneously believes to be his duty?" And the answer here of course is Yes. However, we could regard these principles not as Rules of Life but as what might be called Ideals of Perfection. In that case what we should be interested in is not whether people live by them but whether they live up to them. We should be interested not in what people can reasonably claim to have done but in what they have actually done—and in moral matters these can fall apart.

In which of these two ways are we to regard the principle of Equal Rights—as a Rule of Life or as an Ideal of Perfection? Are we to ask of a man whether he can claim to have abided by it, or whether he really has abided by it? Now, the principle of doing one's duty is part of the "moral education" of human beings: and the point of moral education is to produce good human beings. And the goodness of human beings is determined by the rules that they live by. The principle of Equal Rights, however, is part of the "political education" of statesmen: and the point of "political education," I submit, is not to produce good statesmen but to produce good states. And if the goodness of statesmen is determined by the rules that they live by, the goodness of states is determined by the rules that statesmen live up to. In consequence, though it is reasonable to treat the principle of doing one's duty as a Rule of Life, to treat the principle of equal rights in the same way is to miss its point. Good intentions in a ruler are of little interest except in so far as they augur good results.

At this stage it might be objected that the assertion that everyone has equal rights seems to come to no more than the assertion that everyone has such rights as he has. In the expression "equal rights" the word "equal" occurs vacuously. Now the force of this objection is far from evident. Of course, if everyone's rights are equal, then to attribute to everyone equal rights is to attribute to everyone nothing more than such rights as he has: but conversely, if everyone's rights are equal, to recognize such rights as everyone has, is to recognize nothing less than everyone's equal rights. In other words, if everyone's rights are equal, then the two expressions "everyone's equal rights" and "such rights as everyone has" denote the same thing: but this is not surprising—for this could be false only if the expression "everyone's equal rights" did not denote everyone's equal rights or the expression "such rights as everyone has" did not denote such rights as everyone has. The pertinent question now emerges as, Does the word "equal" in the assertion that everyone has equal rights, add anything to our knowledge of the kind of rights that everyone has?

And the force of the objection that I am considering may lie just here: in, that is to say, the denial of any informative value to the word "equal." Indeed, this denial might be thought to follow from what I have already said. For if in the matter of any single commodity it is in principle possible for two people to have rights to widely different quantities and for these rights to be equal, surely nothing is said by calling these rights equal? But this argument leaves out a vital step. For it will be recalled that according to my reasoning it is not possible for anyone to reconcile inequality of distribution with equality of rights without correlating the differential in distribution with a corresponding differential in some other characteristic which is that on which the content of the right depends. In other words, the principle of equal rights demands that if two people have rights to different quantities of some commodity, then there must be some difference elsewhere that justifies this. And this, it seems to me, is not a trivial point. The fact that advocates of reactionary or bigoted policies can always invent spurious reasons for their discrimination, so far from demonstrating the triviality of the point, seems rather to attest to its importance. As one of the greatest of all moralists has said, "L'hypocrisie est un hommage que le vice rend a la vertu." And if in private life this homage is a piece of pompous and nauseating ceremony, in public matters, though no less aesthetically displeasing, it can play a valuable rôle as a curb on prejudice and reaction.

At this point it might be objected that if the upholder of Equal Rights is maintaining that any difference in content between the rights of any two people depends on and is determined by (has as its necessary and sufficient condition) a difference between them in some general characteristic, he is clearly wrong. For what he says may be true of one kind of right but it could not be true of another kind of right whose existence he has doubtless overlooked. This point can be well brought out by means of a distinction made by Professor H. L. A. Hart in a recent paper:[3] that between General Rights and Special Rights. General Rights are rights that all men possess against all, and possess *qua* men. Special Rights are rights that particular men possess against particular

[3] H. L. A. Hart: "Are there any Natural Rights?" *The Philosophical Review*, Vol. LXIV, No. 2, April, 1955, pp. 183-86.

men, and possess in consequence of some special transaction they have conducted or some special relation in which they stand. An example of a General Right would be the right to free speech: examples of a Special Right would be A's right to a yacht in consequence of B's promise to give him one, or A's right to invest B's money in consequence of B's authorization, or A's right to educate B because B is his son. Now it seems that the upholder of the Equality of Rights is committed to the principle that all rights are general rights. But this clearly is unplausible. For no liberal surely is out to deny, say, A's right to whatever it was that B promised him. Accordingly we need to re-interpret the principle of Equal Rights so as to accommodate these cases and yet not compromise the spirit that informs it. And this can I think be done. For though A's right in the matter of the yacht promised him is a special right, it is a special right which is a consequence of a general right. For everyone has the right to become a promisee. And so we might interpret the principle of Equal Rights as condemning all Special Rights which are not consequential upon General Rights.

And here once again we seem up against the charge of triviality. For, it might be objected, with sufficient ingenuity any Special Right that might be claimed could be claimed as a consequence of a General Right. At this stage all I need say in reply is, first, that, whatever people might say, not every Special Right that might be claimed is in fact a consequence of a General Right; and, secondly, that not every Special Right that might be claimed would be claimed as a consequence of a General Right. Indeed, it seems that the old political doctrine of prescription and "prejudice" against which the theory of Equal Rights was in large measure directed, held as one of its main tenets the self-dependence of Special Rights.[4]

II

I now wish to turn to another and rather more complicated problem in the understanding of the notion of Equality or Equal Rights. This, in contradistinction to the Points I have so far discussed, is not concerned with any general characteristic of Equality but arises solely in a special class of cases: namely, competitive situations in which all competitors

[4] e.g., Edmund Burke, "Speech on a Motion for a Committee to Inquire into the State of the Representation of the Commons in Parliament," 7th May, 1782. *The Writings and Speeches of Edmund Burke* (London n.d.), Vol. 7.

have equal rights. In such situations, as in all competitive situations, it is clearly necessary that there should be some mechanism—either of a natural or of an artificial kind—to control competition and effect distribution. The question then arises, What conditions if any must this mechanism satisfy if the demands of Equality are to be safeguarded? Or to put it another way, Under what circumstances would it be said that the equal rights of the competitors had been infringed by the mere workings of the mechanism of competition?

An example will bring out my meaning. In a political democracy recognition is afforded to the equal rights of all to control legislation. But control of legislation is under nearly all circumstances bound to be a competitive affair; the limiting case being that where all interests and aims within a society are harmonious—harmonious, not identical—and are recognized by all to be harmonious. Accordingly some machinery is required to regulate this competition. The problem then arises, How can we be sure that the mechanism required to regulate the competition for the control of legislation does not in doing so infringe the rights of all to control legislation?

There are two points here that require preliminary investigation. First, it might be held by some that we cannot at the same time claim that all people possess equal rights in a certain field and also allow this to be a proper field for competition. Of course, there may in fact be competition in this field; but we cannot condone it, and so a fortiori cannot approve of any particular method of organizing it. For competition and rights are in their very essence incompatible: if people have rights in a certain direction, any competition in that direction is infringement or violation of those rights.

But this is not true. For there are certain perfectly recognizable cases in which rights hold and competition is permissible. For instance, suppose someone is walking along a street and lets a coin drop out of his pocket, and not realizing what he has done walks on and leaves no trace of his ownership. Now everyone who walks along this same street after him has an equal right to pick up that coin[5]—although in this case the situation is rigorously competitive in that only one person can actually pick up the coin. But the fact of competition does not interfere with the rights. The

[5] By English Law this could be stealing by finding; for the purpose of illustration I am assuming a different legal system under which the finder would be entitled to keep the coin in the circumstances described.

fact that only one person will pick up the coin does not prevent the others from having a right to do so: and when the fortunate person picks it up, it is the coin not a set of rights that he makes off with. By his actions the rights of others may be said to lapse—but only of course to the extent that his also does: what certainly could not be said is that by his actions these other rights are violated or infringed. The view that they are is intimately connected with the familiar view that every right has as its correlative a duty: so that in our example, the right, say, of A to pick up the coin entails a duty on the part of anyone other than A not to interfere with his picking it up—and so *inter alia* the duty of everyone other than A not to pick up the coin for himself. But then it just is not the case that every right implies a duty. Within the law, jurists have carefully worked out the distinction between those that do and those that don't, between rights proper or claims, and liberties or privileges. A, for instance, has the right or claim that another man should stay off his land and the liberty or privilege to go on it himself: correlative to the first kind of right is a duty on the part of others (i.e., the duty not to go on to the land), whereas in the second case there is no correlative duty.[6] And it seems to me that there is in morals a parallel to the lawyer's distinction.

The parallel is, however, not perfect. For to the jurist when A has the right to do a certain action in the limited sense of having a privilege to do it, not only has no-one else any specific duty correlative to this right but nothing that anyone else might do would count as an infringement of the right. Of course, in his efforts to stop A from doing what he has the right to do, B might resort to actions that are infringements of other rights of A—in the sense of claims or rights proper of A—or to actions that are offences or crimes in themselves; but what he could not do—for no-one can—is to touch or harm the right itself. In the example of the coin, B might wrest it from A by threatening him or wounding him or hitting him, but however much harm came to A, throughout the whole "bestial scramble" (to use Professor Broad's delightful phrase) the right of A would remain inviolate.

But here I think the moralist would part company with the jurist. For in the eyes of the moralist—and here I mean just the ordinary man in his moralizing moments—though the mere fact of competition does not

---

[6] See, for instance, W. N. Hohfeld: *Fundamental Legal Conceptions* (New Haven, 1923), pp. 36-50. For the connexion between liberties or privileges and competition I am indebted to H. L. A. Hart, *op. cit.*

infringe the rights of other competitors, there are certain ways of conducting the competition that would seem definitely to do so. The violence that B uses against A in our example would seem to be such a case: if B had just used his sharper eyesight to see the coin first and his longer legs to get there first, the right of A to pick up the coin would have remained intact, though of course his fate—to do without it—would have been the same. In such a case B has no duty correlative to A's right—that is to say, he has no duty to let A do what he has a right to do—but his recognition of A's right does commit him to exercising some restraint upon his own conduct. Our problem is in part to try and find a way of characterizing this restraint. In part, I say advisedly. Because A's right might be infringed not just by the behavior of one person or another but by the workings of certain institutions or the pressure of certain impersonal forces. For this reason I have posed my question more generally and asked what demands we are to make of the mechanism of competition—and by this expression I mean all the arrangements that determine whether any given person succeeds in doing that which he has the right to do.

Now, for my second preliminary point. The problem that I am considering arises in situations where everyone has certain rights, it is impossible for everyone to do what he has a right to do, and so we ask, What sort of mechanism can we devise that will determine unambiguously what people may do and at the same time safeguard the rights of all? There is an immediate resemblance between this problem and the problem of social utility as, for instance, it appears in welfare economics. This latter problem arises out of situations where everyone has certain desires, it is impossible for everyone to have what he desires to have, and so we ask, what sort of mechanism can we devise that will determine unambiguously what people may have and at the same time maximize satisfaction of the desires of all?

Yet despite their immediate resemblance, the two problems are, I am convinced, fundamentally different in character. A decision about the maximization of satisfaction of desires is unlike a decision about the safeguarding of rights, and consequently there is no necessary connexion between the conditions that the mechanism of decision must satisfy in the first case and those that we demand be satisfied in the second case.

Let us call the two kinds of decision Welfare decisions and Rights decisions. Now Welfare decisions are the results of aggregating the desires of individuals. There are of course different methods or systems for carrying out this aggregation—each one claiming to fulfill better than any other certain natural or commonsense demands of rationality —but they all exhibit a common pattern. First, numerical values are assigned in accordance with some principle to the various desires of the individuals: on a primitive system only an individual's first preference is considered, on a more sophisticated system his order of preference is taken into account. These numbers are then operated upon in accordance with whatever method of aggregation is employed, and the resultant is the number of the "social" preference.

Now it is obvious that except in the limiting case of complete social harmony—a case which lies outside the terms of my discussion—the number arrived at by the process of aggregation will be different from at least one of the numbers assigned to the various first preferences of the individuals. It follows from this that if we interpret the procedure of aggregation as a method of recommending a certain social policy, given certain desires, then we must allow that it always recommends, *inter alia,* that the desires of certain individuals be frustrated, or (in the cases where orders of preference are considered) that the desires of certain individuals be partially frustrated. Now this consequence is fatal for the view that Rights decisions are strictly parallel to Welfare decisions: the view, that is, that Rights decisions are the results of aggregating the rights of individuals. For if they were, it would follow that they always recommended, *inter alia,* that the rights of certain individuals be infringed or that the rights of certain individuals be partially infringed. But either interpretation will do. For any recommendation of a policy on the grounds that it infringed merely the rights of certain individuals would be unacceptable: for to say that a policy infringes the rights of certain individuals is to condemn it. While Welfare decisions specify ways of minimising frustration of desires, Rights decisions specify ways of eliminating infringement of rights. And again, any recommendation of a policy on the grounds that it merely partially infringes the rights of certain individuals is not just unacceptable, it is unintelligible: for to say that a policy partially infringes the rights of certain individuals is to talk nonsense. There are degrees of frustration, degrees of satisfaction of a desire: a right is either safeguarded or infringed.

We may see testimony, if of an obscure character, to the true nature of the political problem in Rousseau's famous formulation of it—

"trouver une forme d'association qui défende et protège de toute la force commune la personne et les biens de chaque associé, et par laquelle chacun, s'unissant à tous, n'obéisse pourtant qu'à lui-même, et reste aussi libre qu'auparavant." [7] Rousseau's mistake is to talk of freedom in this connexion. For man's freedom is not unrestricted by his subjection to the laws of the state. Rousseau should, instead, have spoken of rights; for in the state man's rights are, or should be, uninfringed.

After these preparatory remarks I now want to return to my original question—In situations where people have equal rights to do certain actions, and not all people can do these actions, what demands should we make of the mechanism that determines what people may do in order that the rights of all be safeguarded?—and in particular to the problem that is the most famous instance of this, that of Democracy—Everyone has an equal right to control legislation, not everyone can control legislation, what mechanism can be evolved that will determine who controls legislation without any infringement of the rights of all to control legislation?

Discussions of the subject abound in the literature of political thought —particularly since that growth of interest in American political and social experience which dates from the middle of the last century. However, such discussions have often been marred or distorted by neglect of the two points that I have endeavoured to bring out. In the first place, a number of thinkers have been under the impression that the rights of all to control legislation are safeguarded if and only if all succeed in controlling legislation: that mere failure to control it entails that the right has been infringed. We find this assumption in, for instance, Burke, who argues from what would be the absurd consequences of recognizing political rights to the non-existence of such rights.[8] We find the view in the Idealist thinkers, who assert the existence of political rights, and attempt to deny the absurdity of the consequences by arguing that people can control legislation without appearing to do so.[9] And again we find this view in John Stuart Mill who regards the problem of politics (a practical, not a metaphysical problem) as that of finding a way whereby everyone can control legislation. His attitude towards rights

[7] J. J. Rousseau: *Du Contrat Social*, I, ii.
[8] Edmund Burke: "An appeal from the New to the Old Whigs, etc." *The Writings and Speeches of Edmund Burke* (London n.d.), Vol. 4.
[9] Bernard Bosanquet: *The Philosophical Theory of the State* (2nd ed., London, 1910), *passim*.

emerges clearly in *Representative Government* where he regards anyone whose vote has not gone directly to the election of a candidate as disfranchised.[10] Now it may be that certain ways of "eliminating" people's votes do infringe their political rights, do disfranchise them—but it is surely wrong to think that all ways do. Furthermore, if we regard people's political rights as rights to control legislation and not just to elect representatives (as surely we must), then on Mill's view we should equally have to say that anyone whose representative was outvoted on a particular issue, was deprived of his rights, which is surely ludicrous. Proportional Representation may be the only way of securing people's political rights: but if it is so, this does not strictly follow from a mere consideration of the nature of these rights.

Secondly, there has of recent years been an effort by certain thinkers to assimilate the problem of democratic legislation to a "welfare" problem. So for instance Kenneth J. Arrow writes:

In a capitalist democracy, there are essentially two methods by which social choices can be made: voting, typically used to make "political" decisions, and the market mechanism, typically used to make "economic" decisions . . . The methods of voting and the market . . . are methods of amalgamating the tastes of many individuals in the making of social choices.[11]

Now, it is certainly true that we could regard democracy in this light, as a method of maximizing satisfaction of certain desires, i.e., those desires which could be expressed in legislation. And we might then come to support it as a "rational" or "good" form of government, or in Mill's words "the ideally best polity." But such a view and such advocacy is, I think, nowadays rather uncommon. Most supporters of Democracy would hold that men had political rights (i.e., rights in political matters) and argue for Democracy on the grounds that it alone took a true view of these rights, i.e., an egalitarian view. For such people the problem of Democracy would not be "to construct a procedure for passing from a set of known individual tastes to a pattern of social decision-making, the procedure in question being required to satisfy certain natural con-

[10] John Stuart Mill: *Representative Government* (London, 1861), Chapter VII.

[11] Reprinted with permission from Kenneth J. Arrow, *Social Choice and Individual Values*, 1951, John Wiley & Sons, Inc., pp. 1-2. For a similar approach, see D. Black: "On the Rationale of Group Decision-Making," *Journal of Political Economy*, Vol. 56, February, 1948, pp, 23-34, and "Un approccio alla teoria delle decisioni di comitato," *Giornale degli economisti e annali di economica*, Vol. 7, N.S., 1948, pp. 262-84.

ditions," [12] but, as I have already said, to construct a mechanism for passing from a set of individual rights to a pattern of social action which does not infringe those rights.

What conditions, then, must such a mechanism satisfy? My answer, briefly, is that it is impossible to specify these conditions *a priori*. This I shall endeavour to substantiate in two ways: first by consideration of a likely suggestion of what these conditions might be, and secondly on general grounds.

It might be thought that though the task of devising a mechanism for the safeguarding of rights is not the same as that of devising a mechanism for the maximization of satisfaction—in that the specifications on which one would be working would not be the same in the one case as in the other—still the outcome might be the same in that the same mechanism would do for both purposes. And this idea has a great deal of plausibility to it. For we can regard the exercise of a right as always a case of the satisfaction of a desire: so, if, for instance, I exercise my right to pick up a coin in the street, I might be regarded as also satisfying my desire to pick it up. Now it might therefore be thought that the obvious practical interpretation of safeguarding everyone's rights in a certain direction is to maximize the satisfaction of everyone's desires in that direction. No longer would it be thought that the two policies are identical, but it might be held that the one is the obvious way of achieving the other. And indeed the plausibility of this view is well attested to by the all but universal preference of Democracy for Representative Government: for representative government is on the whole a sound method of maximizing satisfaction of wants.[13] Another way of putting this view would be to say that the condition we demand of any mechanism for safeguarding individual rights is that "rationality" which economists demand of any mechanism for aggregating individuals' desires.

[12] Kenneth J. Arrow, *op. cit.*, p. 2.

[13] It does, of course, give rise to some incongruities, e.g. the "paradox of voting" quoted by Arrow, *op. cit.*, pp. 2-3: "Suppose there is a community of three voters, and this community must choose among three alternative modes of social action . . . Let A, B and C be the three alternatives, and 1, 2 and 3 the three individuals. Suppose individual 1 prefers A to B and B to C (and therefore, A to C), individual 2 prefers B to C and C to A (and therefore B to A), and individual 3 prefers C to A and A to B (and therefore C to B). Then a majority prefer A to B, and a majority prefer B to C. We may therefore say that the community prefers A to B and B to C. If the community is to be regarded as behaving rationally, we are forced to say that A is preferred to C. But in fact a majority of the community prefer C to A."

But I think we can see that this will not work by considering an extreme case. Let us suppose that there is a community of a hundred voters who every year must chose from out of a hundred alternative courses of political action the policy for the ensuing year. Let the voters be V_1 ... V_{100} and the courses of action C_1 ... C_{100}. Now every year the poll shows that the political desires within the community are quite static. Regularly V_1 ... V_{99} distribute their first preferences between C_1 ... C_{99} so that every course of action is the first preference of one and only one voter: and regularly V_{100} expresses his first preference for C_{99}. Every voter is indifferent between every course of action other than that preferred. (If we are to take seriously interpersonal comparisons, we must make the further supposition that all voters are equally sensitive.) Now, if we are concerned with the maximization of satisfaction of desires, we should without doubt expect C_{99} to be adopted every year as the policy for the coming year. That would be the "rational" social choice. For the adoption of any other course would clearly produce greater frustration, i.e., it would frustrate ninety-nine voters instead of a mere ninety-eight. However, I think that there is no doubt that if we believe that every voter has a right to select the policy of the community, then we should not be prepared to abide by this decision. We should feel that it infringed the rights of the unsuccessful voters, and that in a situation where the desires of all were so diverse and so evenly distributed between the alternatives, some such mechanism as choice of policy by lot would be fairer.

Now what is this characteristic of "fairness" [14] that we expect of our mechanism? Here we have, I suggest, a clear instance of it in practice, and yet no amount of reflection upon this particular case seems to throw any light upon it as a characteristic. We decide that it is present in one arrangement and absent from another by means of a process that seems to escape all our attempts to formulate it. Experience, and knowledge of the world, and knowledge of human nature, all seem to help us, but we cannot say how.

This inductive argument is confirmed by general considerations. For

---

[14] I think that it will be apparent that the notion of "fairness" that I am discussing has nothing to do with that recently discussed by Professor R. B. Braithwaite in his *Theory of Games as a Tool for the Moral Philosopher* (Cambridge, 1955). For the problems that he is concerned with are a sub-class of welfare problems, i.e., those where collaboration between the competitors is feasible. It is significant that the notion of "rights" finds no place in his vocabulary.

what our mechanism is required to do is to ensure that there is no infringement of anyone's political rights: but political rights are, as we have seen, privileges or liberties, not claims or rights proper: and in consequence non-infringement of them is not a matter of certain specific duties being observed: it is a matter of the competitive system within which they are exercised not being subject to undue interference or coercion. But what amounts to undue interference or coercion seems to be a matter we cannot decide in advance of political experience.

It might indeed justly be thought that the progress of political thought lies in the ever-widening consciousness of new obstacles to the enjoyment of our rights where these compete. At any given moment we may create a mechanism to determine who shall be allowed to do what, which can guard against known threats to liberty: but there is no way of anticipating future discoveries.

III

I have left myself almost no space to say anything about the justification of the principle of Equality or its relation to the other principles of the Liberal tradition. These are of course connected matters, for to ask whether one principle is related to another is to ask whether one entails or is entailed by the other, and to find that one principle is entailed by another is often enough to find its justification, or at any rate *a* justification for it.

My own opinion is that the principle of Equality can be regarded as the fundamental principle of Liberalism. We have seen already how the principle of Democracy can be interpreted as a special instance of it. And the principle of Liberty is made superfluous by it. For the substance of every claim that men should be free in a certain matter could be rendered by claiming that in this matter they have equal rights. And, contrary to an established view, this can be extended outside the sphere of social justice where every assertion of a right is, as it were, a sketch or a demand for a law, to those areas of private life, such as sexual behaviour, where a correct view of these rights demands not the introduction of a law, nor even its reform, but its abolition.

Equality as an Ideal

ISAIAH BERLIN

I

"Every man to count for one and no one to count for more than one." This formula, much used by utilitarian philosophers, seems to me to form the heart of the doctrine of equality or of equal rights, and has coloured much liberal and democratic thought. Like many familiar phrases of political philosophy it is vague, ambiguous, and has changed in connotation from one thinker and society to another. Nevertheless, it appears, more than any other formula, to constitute the irreducible minimum of the ideal of equality. Moreover it is not self-evident in the sense in which many simple empirical propositions seem so; it has not been universally believed; and it is not uniquely connected with any one philosophical system. The notion of each man counting for one and only one, does not depend on belief in rights, either natural or positive, either divinely bestowed or adopted by convention. The statement that each man is to count for one may, of course, be conceived as flowing from the recognition of natural rights possessed by all men as such—rights "inherent" in being a man at all—whether innate, or conferred at birth by a divine act—and so an "inalienable" element in the "ultimate structure" of reality. But equally it can be held without any metaphysical views of this kind. Again, it may be regarded as a rule, whether universal or confined to certain defined classes of persons, deriving its validity from a system of rights based on specific legal enactments, or custom, or some other identifiable source of human authority. But again, it need not depend on this. One can perfectly well conceive of a society organised on Benthamite or Hobbesian lines, in which rights did not exist, or played a small part, and in which the

From the *Proceedings of the Aristotelian Society*, vol. 56 (1955-56). Reprinted by permission of the author and the Aristotelian Society.

principle of "every man to count for one" was rigorously applied for utilitarian reasons, or because such was the will of the despot, or of the majority, or of the legislator or whoever held sovereignty in a given society. It is doubtless true that the most ardent champions of equality were, in fact, believers in human rights in some sense. Some were theists who believed that all men had immortal souls every one of which possessed infinite value and had claims which consequently must not be set aside in favour of objectives of lower value; some of these in addition believed in absolute standards of justice, divinely sanctioned, from which the doctrine of equality was directly deducible. Others were liberals and democrats, some of them deists or atheists or others ignorant of, or opposed to, the Judaeo-Christian tradition, who believed in the principle of equality *a priori,* as being revealed by natural light or whatever other source or method of knowledge was regarded as being the most certain. This was the foundation of the faith of the framers of the declarations of human rights in the American and the French revolutions; and has indeed been perhaps the strongest single element in egalitarian doctrines from the days of the Gracchi to the socialists and anarchists of modern times. But the connection between "counting for one" and the doctrines of Christian theology or the French *philosophes,* or this or that view of reason or of nature is rather more historical and psychological than logical. At any rate it is not one of mutual entailment. For this reason it may be of some use to enquire what this principle will look like if it is detached from its normal historical and psychological setting—whether it possesses any inherent plausibility of its own, and whence it derives its universal and perennial appeal.

I should like to suggest that there is a principle of which the egalitarian formula is a specific application: namely, that similar cases call for, i.e., should be accorded, similar treatment. Then, given that there is a class of human beings, it will follow that all members of this class, namely, men, should in every respect be treated in a uniform and identical manner, unless there is sufficient reason not to do so.[1] But since more than a finite degree of social and personal uniformity is in practice

[1] In this formulation the principle will cover both of the forms of equal rights to property distinguished by Mr. Wollheim, i.e., both absolute equality of property, and equality conditional upon specific qualifications, say, sufficient means to enable a man to buy it, or legal rights of inheritance, and the like. The notion of "sufficient reason" can be made to cover almost any type of situation, and is suspect for that very reason.

difficult or impossible to achieve, the principle ordains that the rule
should be applied in, at any rate, important respects—those respects in
which the type of treatment accorded to each other by human beings
makes a great deal of difference to them, affects them deeply, forwards or
frustrates their desires or interests in a significant degree. The assumption here seems to be that unless there is some sufficient reason not to do
so, it is "natural" or "rational" to treat every member of a given class (in
this case, men) as you treat any one member of it. To state the principle
in this way leaves open crucial issues: thus it may be justly objected that
unless some specific sense is given to "sufficient reason," the principle can
be reduced to a trivial tautology (it is reasonable to act in manner X save
in circumstances Y, in which it is not rational, and *any* circumstances may
be Y); furthermore that since all entities are members of more than one
class—indeed of a theoretically limitless number of classes—*any* kind of
behavior can be safely subsumed under the general rule enjoining equal
treatment—since unequal treatment of various members of class A can
always be represented as equal treatment of them viewed as members of
some other class B, which in extreme circumstances can be so constructed
as to contain no more than one actual member; which can reduce this
rule to vacuity. There obviously can exist no formal method of avoiding
such reductions to absurdity; they can be rebutted only by making clear
what reasons are sufficient and why; and which attributes are alone
relevant and why; and this will depend on the outlooks and scales of
values of different persons, and the purposes of a given association or
enterprise, in terms of which alone general principles can retain any
degree of significance—whether in theory or practice. In concrete cases
we distinguish good reasons from bad, central characteristics from irrelevant ones. Some inequalities (say, those based on birth) are condemned
as arbitrary and irrational, others (say, those based on efficiency) are not,
which seems to indicate that values other than equality for its own
sake affect the ideals even of passionate egalitarians. A part of what we
mean by rationality is the art of applying, and combining, reconciling,
choosing among general principles in a manner for which complete
theoretical explanation (or justification) can never, in principle, be
given.

To return to the principle in the form in which it is normally applied:
if I have a voice in settling the destinies of my society I think it unfair
that all other members of it should not also have a similar voice; if I

own property, it is unfair that others (situated in relevant respects as I am) should not do so too, and if I am allowed to leave it to my children in my will it is unfair that others should not have a similar opportunity; if I am permitted to read or write or express my opinion freely it is wrong, unjust, unfair, etc., that others should not be permitted to do so too. If someone is not to be allowed to do these things, or have these advantages, then sufficient reasons must be given; but no reason need be given for not withholding them, i.e., for an equal distribution of benefits—for that is "natural"—self-evidently right and just, and needs no justification, since it is in some sense conceived as being self-justified. A society in which every member holds an equal quantity of property needs no special justification; only a society in which property is unequal needs it. So too with the distribution of other things—power or knowledge, or whatever else can be possessed in different quantities or degrees. I can justify the fact that the commander of an army is to be given more power than his men by the common purposes of the army, or of the society which it is defending—victory, or self-protection—which can best be achieved by this means; I can justify the allocation of more than an equal share of goods to the sick or the old (to secure equality of satisfactions), or to the specially meritorious (to secure a deliberately intended inequality); but for all this I must provide reasons. If I believe in a hierarchical society, I may try to justify the special powers or wealth or position of persons of a certain origin, or of castes or classes or ranks, but for all this I am expected to give reasons—divine authority, a natural order, or the like. The assumption is that equality needs no reasons, only inequality does so; that uniformity, regularity, similarity, symmetry, the functional correlation of certain characteristics with corresponding rights of which Mr. Wollheim speaks, need not be specially accounted for, whereas differences, unsystematic behaviour, change in conduct, need explanation and, as a rule, justification. If I have a cake and there are ten persons among whom I wish to divide it, then if I give exactly one tenth to each, this will not, at any rate automatically, call for justification; whereas if I depart from this principle of equal division I am expected to produce a special reason. It is some sense of this, however latent, that makes equality an ideal which has never seemed intrinsically eccentric, even though extreme forms of it may not have been wholly acceptable to either political thinkers or ordinary men throughout recorded human history. There seem to me to be at least two conceptions which are involved in this love of order, each of which Mr. Wollheim has touched upon (although not by name or directly). These are the notions (a) of rules, and (b) of equality proper. I should like to say something about each of these.

(A) *Rules*. All rules, by definition, entail a measure of equality. In so far as rules are general instructions to act or refrain from acting in certain ways, in specified circumstances, enjoined upon persons of a specified kind, they enjoin uniform behaviour in identical cases. To fall under a rule is *pro tanto* to be assimilated to a single pattern. To enforce a rule is to promote equality of behaviour or treatment. This applies whether the rules take the form of moral principles and laws, or codes of positive law, or the rules of games or of conduct adopted by professional associations, religious organisations, political parties, wherever patterns of behaviour can be codified in a more or less systematic manner. The rule which declares that tall persons are permitted to cast five times as many votes as short ones creates an obvious inequality. Nevertheless, in the framework of this inequality it ensures equality of privilege within each of the two discriminated classes—no tall man may have more votes than any other tall man, and similarly with short men. This is Mr. Wollheim's first sense of "equality," in which, although the commodities or liberties, be they power or property or status, may not be owned in equal quantities or to an equal degree by everyone, yet every member of each class has an equal right to that which has been accorded to the class as a whole. This type of equality derives simply from the conception of rules as such—namely, that they allow of no exceptions. Indeed what is meant by saying that a given rule exists is that it should be fully, i.e., equally fully, obeyed by those who fall under it, and that any inequality in obedience would constitute an exception, i.e., an offence against the rules. In so far as some minimum degree of prevalence of rules is a necessary condition for the existence of human societies (and this seems to be an almost universal, but still empirical, law), and in so far as morality, both personal and political, is largely conceived of in terms of rules, the kind of equality with which obedience to rules is virtually identical, is among the deepest needs and convictions of mankind. In this sense equality is co-extensive with social morality as such—that is to the degree to which social morality is conceived as a system of coherent, i.e., not internally contradictory (and, according to some moralists, mutually entailing) sets of rules. A plea for equality in this sense is therefore a plea for life in accordance with rules as opposed to other standards, e.g., the *ad hoc* orders of an inspired leader, or arbitrary desires. In this sense, then, to say that inequality is wrong is, in effect, to say that it is wrong to obey no rules in a given situation, or to accept a rule and break it; and a situation in which some men, for no stated reason, and in accordance with no rule, consistently obtain more than other men with the same, or sufficiently similar, relevant characteristics (however this is determined) is then described as being unfair. To provide no reasons for breaking a rule is described as irrational; to give reasons for obeying rules—save in terms of other rules—is regarded as unnecessary—rules are their own justification. In a moral system which entirely consists of rules, and is definable in terms of them, adequate reasons for breaking rule X must take the form of rule Y, which in certain circumstances may come into collision with Rule X, and, in accordance with Rule Z, will then cancel or modify it or, at any rate, be allowed to do so. A society which accepts a morality, whether personal or social and political, analysable into sets of rules of varying orders of stringency, some independent of each other, some connected by relations of entailment or mutual exclusion, may then be open to at least three kinds of criticism.

1. I may accept the rules, and complain that too many exceptions are being made without specific rules to back the exceptions. If I merely object to the exceptions as such, I am merely complaining of the infringement of moral or social laws, as such. If the exceptions fulfil the desires of some people to the detriment of the fulfilment of the desires of others—for example where the desires are for some commodity in scarce supply, be it property, or power or status, or the fruits of civilisation, then, if there is no rule governing such distribution (or if there is a rule but exceptions to it are made arbitrarily, i.e., without being deducible from, or justifiable in terms of, other accepted rules) I complain, in addition, of unfairness, i.e., that similar cases are being treated dissimilarly, when the whole essence of the rules is that this should be avoided.

2. I may complain that the rules themselves are bad or iniquitous. This may take several forms: I may complain that a given rule offends against some other rule or principle which seems to me more important or morally superior. A rule consistently favouring the tall as against the short, would offend against the rule which I regard as superior, accord-

ing to which physical characteristics must not be considered in, let us
say, the distribution of honours; or against a rule which lays it down
that all men, or all Englishmen, or all members of the Aristotelian
society, must be treated as being equal in this regard. Then again
someone may say that equal treatment only for members of the Aristotelian society offends against equal treatment for all Englishmen, or
that equal treatment for all Englishmen offends against the principle of
equal treatment for all Europeans, or all men. In short, a rule may be
condemned as offending against some wider rule to which it is then
regarded as forming an irrational exception. Or it may be attacked on
the ground that it conflicts with some rule not necessarily wider but
merely incompatible with it; in cases of such conflict egalitarianism
seems to entail that any rule which includes under it a larger number
of persons or a larger number of types of persons[2] shall always be
preferred to rules which ensure identical treatment only for smaller
numbers or a smaller number of types; and a society will not be egalitarian to the degree to which in the formulation of its rules, or in its
system of deciding which rules win in cases of conflict, it is influenced
by principles other than those of the intrinsic desirability of identical
treatment of the largest possible numbers of persons or classes of persons; for example if it is bent on the maximisation of happiness, which
way well entail gross inequalities.[3] And of course there are many other
goals or values which may deflect the course of strict egalitarianism, as,
for instance, the desire to encourage the arts and sciences, or a pre-
dominant desire to increase the military or economic power of the state,
or a passion for the preservation of ancient traditions, or a strong taste
for change and variety and new forms of life. All these may or may not
breed rules that conflict with the principle that every man is to count

[2] A policy of equal treatment for the largest number of persons may easily conflict
with a policy of equal treatment of the largest number of classes of persons. Thus a
reformer bent on abolishing discriminatory legislation may find himself faced with
a choice between incommensurables, e.g., of emancipating either one large class of
"inferiors," say, the poor, or several such classes, say, religious or racial minorities,
which between them contain fewer members than the single large class. The first
policy will give equality to more human beings; the second will abolish a greater
number of class distinctions. Since either course can correctly be said to increase
equality, and both cannot (for some practical reason) be adopted, the choice of a
conscientious egalitarian will depend on the type of equality preferred. As it stands
the question before him cannot be answered.
[3] With the exception, I suppose, of those societies in which the desire for equality
is itself so much stronger than all other desires, that inequality automatically breeds
greater misery than any other possible arrangement.

for one and only one. This principle will indeed be preserved by the mere existence of rules within each area dominated by the rules themselves; but rules cannot guarantee its extension each beyond its own field. For the rules themselves may create inequalities, and the conflict between the rules still greater ones. To say, as we often do of a rule, that it is itself unfair, is, in effect, to say that it contradicts some other rule with a wider area of equal treatment—a rule which, if obeyed, will ensure that a larger number of persons (or classes of persons) shall receive similar treatment in specified circumstances. But to say of the rule that it is bad or iniquitous need not mean this; it need mean only that it is in conflict with some other rule or principle not necessarily itself tending towards greater equality. In case this seems too abstract, let me illustrate: although Bentham's doctrine about each man to count for one was in fact embodied by him in his utilitarian teachings, it seems plain that equality is not itself entailed by utilitarian principles, and might, indeed, on occasion conflict with them. Thus it can be argued that societies organised hierarchically, certain types of mediaeval society, for example, or theocratic societies or even societies founded on slavery, may conceivably offer their members a greater degree of happiness (however this is calculated) than societies in which there is a greater degree of social or economic equality. When Montesquieu or Rousseau, for example, declare that the objection to slavery is not that it makes men unhappy—for it may not—the slaves may prefer to remain slaves— but that it is slavery, that men have no right to enslave other men, that it is unworthy of human beings to create such forms of life, they are pleading for equality for equality's sake. They are in effect saying that any society which has rules or laws enjoining or permitting slavery, even though its members may be happier than if they had been free, and even though Aristotle may be right and men exist whose faculties are realised best in slavery, is yet a society to be condemned, not for breaking the rules under which it lives, but for obeying the wrong kind of rules, pursuing the wrong kind of values. And this implies that equality, that is to say, the rule that each man is to count for one and for no more than one, whether in the distribution of property or in the number of votes he has in the sovereign assembly, or in the opportunities for education or pleasure, or in whatever respect, is an end in itself, in possible conflict with other ends, but higher than they, and, in cases of conflict, to be preferred.

3. Finally, someone may attack a society not indeed for breaking the rules that it affects to respect; nor yet for living by rules that are bad, or in conflict with some other ends or ideals which the critic regards as of greater moral authority; but that it lives by rules at all, that it is rule ridden. And if it is pointed out to him that a certain minimum of rules is an empirical necessity for the preservation of any degree of human organisation, then he may retreat to the position that the rules in use go far beyond this minimum, and that a morality not compounded out of rules, but consisting of the pursuit of some ideal in a spontaneous and imaginative way, analogous to the creative activity of a painter or a composer, or to even less disciplined forms of self-expression, where both the use and recognition of rules is at a minimum, is to be preferred. It is salutary to be reminded that moral and political outlooks are not co-extensive with systems of moral or political rules. The Romantic attack upon the moral systems both of rationalists and empiricists at times took precisely this form of denunciation of the propositions and imperatives of the classical ethical systems, not because they were mistaken or deleterious, but because they were general. The Romantic philosophers, particularly in Germany,[4] assailed their predecessors for imposing rules, amalgamating cases, whether individual characters or moral situations or moral actions, that were necessarily unique and incommensurable, under the umbrella of some universal formula. They attacked all those who seemed to them bent on forcing the teeming multiplicity and variety of human activity into a Procrustean bed of symmetrical sets of moral rules, which, precisely because they were rules, tended to represent differences as being relatively unimportant, and similarities as being alone relevant; and especially those who, so it was maintained, by following a false analogy with the natural sciences, ignored, or misrepresented vital individual differences, in virtue of which alone things and persons possessed their unique value, and did this in order to achieve an egalitarian society, dominated by rules— a society directed against the existence of all those elements which the Romantics regarded as alone worth preserving.

All three types of attack upon a given social or political order are, to say the least, relevant to the belief in equality. Let me recapitulate them: they take the form of saying—

---

[4] This, or something like it, was also advocated by M. Bergson in one of his last works—that on the *Two Sources of Morality and Religion.*

(a) that rules are broken for no sufficient reason; or

(b) that the rules are themselves bad or iniquitous or otherwise inadequate; or

(c) that the rules are deplorable simply because they are rules.

Of these (a) represents the most direct demand for equality, for any protest against exceptions, because they are exceptions, is a genuine plea for equality; (b) springs from a demand for equality only if the rules are attacked on the ground that they are in conflict with other rules aimed at producing a greater degree of general equality; (c) is a direct attack upon the ideal of social equality as such. It is clear that this ideal is not solely the equality which all rules entail as such (even though it may derive much force from an intimate connexion with moral systems to which universality, order, rules, laws, etc., are central), since otherwise rules could not themselves be criticized as leading to inequality, as we have seen that they can be. What then is this ideal?

II

(B) *Equality proper.* In its simplest form the ideal of complete social equality embodies the wish that everything and everybody should be as similar as possible to everything and everybody else. It may serve to make this concept clearer if we try to conceive of some of the characteristics of a world in which no type of egalitarian would have anything to complain of. I doubt whether anyone has ever seriously desired to bring such a society into being, or even supposed such a society to be capable of being created. Nevertheless, it seems to me that the demands for human equality which have been expressed both by philosophers and by men of action who have advocated or attempted to reform society, can best be represented as modifications of this absolute and perhaps absurd ideal. In the ideal egalitarian society, inequality—and this must ultimately mean dissimilarity—would be reduced to a minimum. The greatest single cause of complaint has been disparity in the possession, or enjoyment, of characteristics or commodities which have been strongly desired by men at most times—such as property, political or social power, status, opportunities for the development of faculties or the obtaining of experiences, social and personal liberties and privileges of all kinds. And the attack has taken the form of maintaining that a society in which some men are much richer or stronger or freer than

others; in which some men possess the power of acquiring what they
want and of preventing others from acquiring these same things or
other things which they in turn want; or in which some men are paid
homage and deferred to and permitted to live as they wish in ways
and degrees which set them off from other men; all these are societies
which offend either against the principle of natural rights, which according to those who hold this principle, belong to all men as such; or
against some rational principles whereby these differences may indeed
be justified, but only by the provision of sufficient reasons for instituting
or maintaining them. Disputes occur about what these rights are; or
what reasons are sufficient or good; and whether such characteristics as
differences of birth or of colour or of religion or of wealth are true
sources of unequal rights, or furnish good reasons for instituting political
or social or other similar inequalities. There is, of course, a significant
difference between these two ways of approach. Those who believe in
natural rights differ mainly in establishing what these rights are, how
their existence can be verified, whether all of them belong to all men,
or only some to all, or only some to some; and whether equality is
desirable in fields other than those covered by the claims created by the
existence of natural rights. The other school—those who appeal to
reason (though historically their views have overlapped with and become inextricably mingled with those of the believers in natural rights)
if they are to be consistent, must believe that equality should stretch
over the entire field of human relations, and be modified only when
there is sufficient reason to do so. Then disagreement may arise as to
what constitutes a sufficient reason, and how great a modification a
given reason justifies, and so forth. The first school, if it is consistent, will
not object to inequalities, providing these do not infringe natural rights.
But the second must protest against any inequality, unless a sufficient
reason for it is produced. It is the latter, therefore, who go further, and
are nearer to the extreme ideal which I should now like briefly to mention. Apart from the crucial question of what are and what are not
sufficient reasons in such cases, it seems plain that inequalities of wealth
or power are merely some among the possible inequalities which can
excite opposition; they tend to be so prominent because they matter—
affect human lives—more deeply, as things are, than other forms of
inequality. But this is not always necessarily so. Even the most convinced social egalitarian does not normally object to the authority

wielded by, let us say, the conductor of an orchestra. Yet there is no obvious reason why he should not. And there have been occasions— few and far between—when this has actually happened. Those who maintain that equality is the paramount good, may not wish to be fobbed off with the explanation that the purpose of orchestral playing will not be served if every player is allowed equal authority with the conductor in deciding what is to be done. Inequality in the organisation of an orchestra there patently is; the reason for it is the purpose of orchestral playing—the production of certain sounds in certain ways which cannot, in fact, be achieved without a measure of discipline which itself entails some degree of inequality in the distribution of authority. But a fanatical egalitarian could maintain that the inequality of the players in relation to the conductor is a greater evil than a poor performance of a symphonic work, and that it is better that no symphonic music be played at all if a conductorless orchestra is not feasible, than that such an institution should be allowed to offend against the principle of equality. To be more serious, the unequal distribution of natural gifts is a well-known obstacle to economic equality: in societies where there is a high degree of equality of economic opportunity, the strong and able and ambitious and cunning are likely to acquire more wealth or more power than those who lack these qualities. The fanatical egalitarian will look on this with horror; and because differences of natural talent will always tend towards the creation of inequalities, if only of prestige or influence, he will consequently wish—if equality is the paramount goal—to root out the evil at the source. He will tend to wish so to condition human beings that the highest degree of equality of natural properties is achieved, the greatest degree of mental and physical, that is to say, total uniformity—which alone will effectively preserve society, as far as possible, from the growth of inequalities of whatever kind. Only in a society where the greatest degree of similarity between the members occurs—where physical characteristics, mental endowment, emotional disposition, and conduct, are as uniform as possible— where people differ as little as possible from each other in any respect whatever, will true equality be attainable. Only in such a society will it be possible to reduce to a minimum those differences of treatment, or of power, or of position, or of natural or acquired characteristics, that are liable to lead people to complain that they have not what others have, and to ask for reasons why this should be so. It may be that the creation of so uniform a society, whether or not it is intrinsically desirable, may not, in fact, be feasible. It may also be that even the attempt to approach it as closely as is humanly possible, requires a degree of radical reorganisation which cannot be carried out without a highly centralized and despotic authority—itself the cause of the maximum of inequality. Some convinced egalitarians have, as everyone knows, in practice accepted this as unavoidable, and have defended the institution of violent inequalities and the total suppression of many normal human claims as a necessary prerequisite for the creation of an ultimate equality. The moral and practical value of this is not relevant to the issue before us. What seems worth emphasising is that so long as there are differences between men, some degree of inequality may occur; and that there is no kind of inequality against which, in principle, a pure egalitarian may not be moved to protest, simply on the ground that he sees no reason for tolerating it, no argument which seems to him more powerful than the argument for equality itself— equality which he regards not merely as an end in itself, but as *the* end, the principal goal of human life. I do not suppose that extreme equality of this type—the maximum similarity of a body of all but indiscernible human beings—has ever been consciously put forward as an ideal by any serious thinker. But if we ask what kinds of equality have in fact, been demanded, we shall see, I think, that they are specific modifications of this absolute ideal, and that it therefore possesses the central importance of an ideal limit or idealized model at the heart of all egalitarian thought.

To examine some of these modifications. There are those who believe that natural human characteristics either cannot or should not be altered and that all that is necessary is equality of political and juridical rights. Provided that there exists equality before the law, such normal democratic principles as that of one man one vote, some form of government arrived at by consent (actual or understood) between the members of the society, or at any rate the majority of them, and, finally, a certain minimum of liberties—commonly called civil liberties—deemed necessary in order to enable men freely to exercise the legal and political rights entailed by this degree of equality, then, according to this view, no interference in other regions of activity (say, the economic) should be permitted. This is a common liberal doctrine of the last century. If it is complained that in a society where a large degree of political and legal equality is ensured, the strong and the clever and the ambitious may succeed in enriching themselves, or acquiring political power, "at the expense of"—that is to say, in such a way as to keep these goods from—other members of the society, and that this leads to patent inequalities, liberals of this school reply that this is the price for ensuring political and legal equality, and that the only method of preventing economic or social inequalities is by reducing the degree of political liberty or legal equality between men. This amounts to an admission that we must choose one of several ways of treating men as counting for only one; that they can be "counted for one" only in some respects, but not in others. For we are told, with considerable empirical evidence, that to count men for one and only one in every respect whatever, is impracticable, that the full degree of, let us say, legal and political equality often results in economic and other forms of inequality, given the different endowments of men, and that only in an absolutely uniform, robot-like society, which no one wants, can this be effectively prevented. Those who believe this commonly maintain that the only inequality which should be avoided is an inequality based on characteristics which the individual cannot alter—unequal treatment based, for instance, on birth, or colour, which human beings cannot alter at will. Given that all human beings start off with equal rights to acquire and hold property, to associate with each other in whatever ways they wish, to say whatever they will, and all the other traditional objectives of liberalism, and with no special rights or privileges attached to birth, colour and other physically unalterable characteristics, then even though some human beings, by skill or luck or natural endowment, do manage to acquire property or power or ascendancy which enables them to control the lives of others, or to acquire objects which the others are not in a position to acquire, then, since there is nothing in the constitution of the society that actually forbids such acquisitiveness, the principle of equality has not been infringed. This is a pure form of *laissez faire* society which its proponents freely admit may lead to inequalities, but defend upon the ground that it gives an equal opportunity to all, a career genuinely open to all the talents—whereas any attempt to secure a greater degree of ultimate equality can only be obtained by interfering with this initial equalisation of opportunity for all. In effect, this is, of course, tantamount to a plea for liberty at the expense of total equality; for it is only pure anarchists who believe that the maximum degree of liberty is wholly compatible with the maximum degree of equality in all important respects, and are called mistaken or utopian to the degree to which this proposition has in fact been falsified by experience. The distinction between general rights and special rights of which Professor H. L. A. Hart has spoken[5] and to which Mr. Wollheim refers, seems to be relevant to this kind of belief. One could easily conceive of a society in which all special rights (rights based on contract or on paternity, for example) will be instances of general rights—particular cases of them—because in such a society, at least in theory, any member can enter into a contract, any member can be a father, any member can enrich himself. There are no rights which belong to individuals in virtue of some characteristics—birth or blood or colour—which other members cannot in principle possess. In this schema certain types of traditional inequality have certainly been ruled out. But to maintain that this is the kind of society that true egalitarians desire would be disingenuous; for if one asks why some types of equality are protected in this case, initial equality whereby all men start off theoretically equal, while other types of equality are not protected, e.g., economic or social equality—equality in respect of whatever men can acquire by their own efforts, the answer is that the criterion of equality has plainly been influenced by something other than the mere desire for equality as such, namely, desire for liberty or the full development of human resources, or the belief that men deserve to be as rich or as powerful or as famous as they can make themselves—beliefs which are not connected with the desire for equality at all.

It is at this point that it becomes clear that in considering what kind of society is desirable, or what are "sufficient reasons" for either demanding equality or, on the contrary, modifying it or infringing it in specific cases, ideals other than equality conspicuously play a vital role.

This is clearly noticeable even in the writings of the most impassioned champions of the widest possible equality. Almost every argument favourable to equality, and in particular the assumption that everything that is scarce should be distributed as equally as possible unless there is strong reason against it, is to be found in the writings of Condorcet. The doctrine of equality in the Declaration of the Rights of Man and Citizen which heralded the French Revolution owes at least as much to him as it does to Rousseau or other thinkers. Yet even Condorcet contemplates the necessity for the government of human beings by men of enlightenment, above all by experts, men versed in the new, not yet created sciences of the behaviour of men—sociology, anthropology and psychology—who alone can create an organisation in which the greatest number of the desires of rational men will not be frustrated, as they have been hitherto, by prejudice, superstition, stupidity and vice. Yet this élite is plainly to have greater powers than those whom they are to govern disinterestedly. And the reason for this is not merely that without this true equality cannot be achieved for the majority of men, but also that certain other ends must be striven for, such as happiness, virtue, justice, progress in the arts and sciences, the satisfaction of various moral and spiritual wants, of which equality, of whatever kind, is only one. Condorcet does not himself seem to be troubled by the problem of whether the quest for equality will clash with the need to seek these other ends, for, in common with many thinkers of his day, he took it for granted all too easily that all good things were certainly compatible, and indeed interlocked, with each other. We need not go into the reasons for this peculiar belief which has dominated much western thought at all times. While the principal assumption which underlies it is the view that since political and moral questions are factual in character, they are each answered by one true proposition and one only (otherwise they are not genuine questions); and since no true propositions can be inconsistent with one another, all the propositions which describe what should be done (no logical distinction is drawn between normative and descriptive statements by these thinkers) must be compatible with one another, and in the perfect harmony which Nature is thought to be, not merely compatible, but mutually entailing and entailed—for that defines a system, and Nature is known *a priori* to be such a—indeed *the*—harmonious system.

Whether or not this is the correct explanation of this central assumption, Condorcet did not allow the possibility of a collision between various human ends. It was left to others to emphasise the fact that in life as normally lived, the ideals of one society and culture clash with those of another, and at times come into conflict within the same society and, often enough, within the moral experience of a single individual; that such conflicts cannot always, even in principle be wholly resolved; that this can be traced to empirical causes, and does not entail either such theological doctrines as those of original sin, or the relevant beliefs

of Buddhist doctrines, nor yet such pessimistic views of human character
as those of Hobbes or Schopenhauer, or the ideologies of modern irrationalism. It follows that when the pursuit of equality comes into conflict with other human aims, be they what they may—such as the desire
for happiness or pleasure, or for justice or virtue, or colour and variety
in a society for their own sake, or for liberty of choice as an end in
itself, or for the fuller development of all human faculties, it is only the
most fanatical egalitarian that will demand that such conflicts invariably
be decided in favour of equality alone, with relative disregard of the
other "values" concerned.

III

Equality is one value among many: the degree to which it is compatible with other ends depends on the concrete situation, and cannot
be deduced from general laws of any kind; it is neither more nor less
rational than any other ultimate principle; indeed it is difficult to see
what is meant by considering it either rational or non-rational.

Yet the principle that every man shall count for one and no more
than one demands a little more consideration before we finally abandon
it as one of the ends pursued by men, needing neither explanation nor
justification, being itself that which explains other rules or ethical principles. It seems, as we have seen above, intimately bound up with the
belief in general rules of conduct. This belief may rest upon religious
or metaphysical or utilitarian grounds, or derive from the love of order
or system as such. However that may be, it often takes the form of a
demand for fairness. The notions of equality and fairness are closely
bound up: if as a result of breaking a rule a man derives benefits which
he can obtain only so long as other men do not break but keep the
rule, then no matter what other needs are being served by such a breach,
the result is an offence against a principle best described as that of fairness, which is a form of desire for equality for its own sake. If I enter a
train and do not pay for my ticket, and conceal this fact from the conductor and the other passengers, and give the sum withheld to a pauper
whose situation is thereby improved materially, it may be argued that
at any rate from a utilitarian point of view I have done what is right. The
railway company will not know of its loss; nor would so small a loss
noticeably decrease "its" happiness; I possess a strong will and shall not
fall into bad habits; the collector has not noticed that he was not paid,

and will not even so much as suffer from a sense of failure to carry out his duties; the passengers in their ignorance will not be led into temptation and demoralisation, nor will there ensue any weakening of confidence between the persons concerned in the transaction leading, in the end, to the discontinuance of the train service. The general sum of happiness—in this case *via* that of the subsidised pauper—will surely have gone up to a greater degree than if I had paid my fare to the train conductor. Nevertheless, quite apart from the morally relevant fact that, having entered into a quasi-contractual obligation to pay, I have broken my promise, my act would be condemned as unfair, for it would rightly be maintained that I can only gain advantage (or the pauper can only gain advantage) so long as the other passengers continue to behave as they did before—since if my act were generally followed no one would pay, and the trains would stop running. So long as my advantage directly depends on the fact that others continue to obey the rule which applies to me as much as to them, so that I alone profit by the exception which I have made in my own favour, such a relaxation of the rule for my benefit would be rightly stigmatised as unfair (as well as dishonest); and although critical situations can be easily imagined in which it would be morally better that I should act in this way and break my contract, or cheat, yet it is clear that a person of normal moral sensitiveness would cheat in this manner only with considerable qualms—qualms derived not merely from the fact that he has broken a contract, but from the sense of the unfairness of what he was doing. Indeed liability to such qualms is among the very criteria of what we call moral sensitiveness. If, despite them, a man resolved to commit such an act, his moral justification would necessarily take the form of invoking, and attempting to balance the claims of, ends or values other than those of equality. He would be drawn in one direction by such considerations as the sanctity of promises; the social need to keep one's word and preserve the rule of law and the social order; the intrinsic desirability of avoiding unfairness; and so on. These factors he would have to weigh against such others as the desirability of increasing happiness (in this case of the pauper) or of avoiding the creation of misery; the claims, say, of scientific curiosity; the desire to follow some romantic impulse or vision of life, and so on. And the same kind of considerations will apply when exceptions are made to rules for "good" or "sufficient" reasons. The goodness of the reasons will depend upon the degree of value or importance attached to the purposes or motives adduced in justifying the exceptions, and these will vary as the moral convictions—the general outlooks—of different individuals or societies vary. I may consider it right to reward ability and achievement, and not, for example, honesty and kindness when they are accompanied by stupidity or ineptitude or failure. But others may well think this wrong, and the opposite morally right. I may think it right to reward the bearers of celebrated names or the descendants of famous families as such; or to deny certain rights to negroes which I grant freely to Englishmen; and may try to defend this policy by maintaining that a society in which this is the normal practice seems to me intrinsically better, or more stable, or accords more closely with some pattern sanctioned by my religion, or my metaphysical beliefs about the structure of the universe, or the laws of history, whereas you will reject a society dedicated to such practices as iniquitous because, let us assume, you reject my religion, or my metaphysics; or because you believe me to be interpreting them falsely, or think that a society constructed on such principles is intrinsically bad, or politically precarious; or simply because you believe so passionately in equality for its own sake, that you are not deterred by the realization that the consequences which I (and perhaps you too) wish to avert may well be brought about by opposing my policies. There are many ways in which such basic disagreements can manifest themselves: one man or sect or political party may desire equality in one sphere of life, say in social or in legal relationships or legal status, and ignore the economic consequences; another may regard economic relationships as being supremely important, and be prepared to tolerate lack of social or legal equality for the sake of a given economic structure. Some may regard exceptions made in favour of specific gifts or genius as justifiable by social results. Others may regard this as unfair, but, in their turn, believe in some natural social hierarchy, like Burke, and demand full equality of treatment upon each rung of the ladder—the only "true" equality—but bitterly oppose as being contrary to the natural order any attempt to deny the existence or relevance of such rungs or hierarchies, with its accompaniment of demands for equal treatment for all.[6] Consequently when, as often

---

[6] Or, like Plato and Aristotle, insist only on the natural hierarchy and appropriate differences of treatment at each level, without apparently caring whether there is social or economic equality between inhabitants of the same level, implying clearly that within each class unbridled competition can take place. Classical thought seems to be deeply and "naturally" inegalitarian.

happens, a man admits that a law is administered fairly—that is to say with due regard to the principle of equality—but complains that the law itself is bad or iniquitous, we cannot always be clear about what is meant. The critic may wish to say that the more fairly the law in question is administered, the more this frustrates a principle of wider equality in which he himself believes, as when a law based upon the principle of discrimination between coloured and white men is administered fairly, i.e., with scrupulous regard to equal treatment within each category, but is thereby itself the cause of inequality between coloured and white men. But the critic may have other reasons for complaint. He may attack this law because it offends against some value other than equality— because it promotes misery, because it frustrates talent, because it makes for social instability, because it insists upon equality in what the attacker thinks unimportant matters, but ignores equality in what he regards as more important aspects of human life (the scale of importance being decided in terms of values other than equality itself); because it ignores the claims of a religion; because it fulfils the claims of religion; because it is obscure or vague or too difficult to obey; and for an infinity of other possible reasons. Very commonly, because as in the instance given above, it permits one kind of equality at the expense of another, which can be a matter of fine nuance. In Mr. Wollheim's very ingenious example, where all the members of a community have equal rights and one vote per head, and each votes for some end different from those of the others, but two members by constantly voting in the same way are enabled theoretically to overrule all the others, what we object to is not the inequality of such a system, for in legal and even in political, terms, complete equality is clearly ensured. The unfairness of which Mr. Wollheim speaks is caused by our recognition that in this situation too great a majority of the voters find themselves permanently frustrated; we desire to see some degree of equality, not only of choices but of satisfactions, and regard it as "fairer" if some system of chance, e.g., lot, were adopted, which by equalizing the chances of success, would prevent, at any rate, this type of systematic dissatisfaction. We should regard a system in which each person were permitted to have "his day" as fairer still. This is a typical clash between two systems incompatible in practice, each of which can claim to promote equality; one in the matter of the machinery of self-government, the other in the matter of the distribution of rewards. Similarly there is a conflict between those

for whom equality means non-discrimination in fields of human activity
deemed important (however these are identified) on the basis of unalterable characteristics, e.g., origins or physical characteristics, and the
like, and those who reject this as an inadequate criterion and desire
equality of treatment to remain unaffected even by such "alterable"
attributes as religious or political views, personal habits and the like.
We seem to choose as we choose because one solution seems to us to
embody a blend of satisfaction of claims and desires (or to contain or
omit other factors) which we prefer as a total pattern to the blend
provided by the other solution. Indeed the intervention of considerations
of equity in the rigorous workings of some deductive legal system are
due to our desire for justice that we are not always able to analyse too
closely, into which the principle of "every man to count for one" does
indeed enter, but without any clear understanding whether he is to
count for one in the sphere of legislative rights, or of responsibility for
action, or the receipt of benefits, or other respects, between any of which
conflict all too easily occurs. And, of course, even in matters of equity
the "counting for one" principle is, as often as not, modified by other
ends and beliefs, in whatever combination they occur in a given culture
or ethical system or within the outlook of an individual thinker.

Finally, those must not be forgotten who, as was said above, object to
all rules as such and desire a society, whether this is practicable or not,
governed in an unsystematic manner by the will of an inspired leader,
or by the unpredictable movement of the Volksgeist, or the "spirit" of a
race, a party, a church. This amounts to rejection of rules, and of
equality as an end valuable in itself, and it is as well to recognise that
this attitude is not as rare or as ineffective as liberal and socialist thinkers
have sometimes assumed. In its conflicts with the traditional western
principles of equality or justice or natural rights, or that minimum of
civil liberties which is required to protect human beings from degrada-
tion and exploitation, romantic irrationalism has at times won easily
enough. I cite this only as a warning against the thesis that the com-
mandment to treat all men alike in like situations needs no independent
argument to support it, and that the proper criteria for what constitutes
likeness cannot be doubted or conflict with each other, but are something
taken for granted by reasonable men, a form of the working of natural
reason which needs no justification, but is as self-evident as the principle
of identity or that red is different from green. This is far from being so;

and the vicissitudes of liberal principles in the last, and especially this, century, seem partly due to the unwarranted assumption on the part of their defenders that those who reject these principles only do so through ignorance or intellectual indolence or mental perversity or blindness.[7] Belief in equality—fairness—the view that unless there is a reason for it, recognized as sufficient by some identifiable criterion, one man should not be preferred to another, is a deep-rooted principle in human thought. It has been assimilated into many systems, those of the utilitarians and the theories of natural right, as well as various religious doctrines, but can be isolated from them, and has entered them less by way of logical connection, than by psychological affinity or because those who believed in these utilitarian or religious or metaphysical doctrines also in fact— perhaps from a craving for symmetry and unity that is at the root of all these views—believed in equality for its own sake, and therefore considered any society which did not make sufficient room for this principle to be to that degree worth less than one that did. In its extreme form egalitarianism requires the minimisation of all differences between men, the obliteration of the maximum number of distinctions, the greatest possible degree of assimilation and uniformity to a single pattern. For all differences are capable of leading to irregularities of treatment. If this ideal is on the whole rejected in actual political doctrines, this seems mainly due to the fact that it conflicts with other ideals with which it cannot be wholly reconciled; indeed most ethical and political views are forms of less or more uneasy compromise between principles which in their extreme form cannot co-exist.

[7] As, for instance, by Locke, when in the *Second Treatise of Government*, he says "nothing more evident than that creatures of the same species and rank promiscuously born to all the same advantages of nature and the use of the same faculties, should also be equal one amongst another." This is the equality that the judicious Hooker is then praised for regarding as "evident in itself, and beyond all question." This, of course, is the pure doctrine of Natural Law, which Locke himself questioned (in the same year) in the *Essay* where he tells us that "there cannot any one moral rule be proposed whereof a man may not justly demand a reason" and contrasts "that most unshaken rule of morality and foundation of all social virtue, 'That one should do as he would be done unto'" which can "without any absurdity" be questioned and "a reason why?" demanded—with such genuinely senseless questions as why "it is impossible for the same thing to be and not to be." Locke's hesitations and confusions mark the beginning of the breakdown of the notion that at least some moral or political principles are as self-evident as those of logic or that "red is different from blue." An excellent discussion of this and related topics is to be found in Professor Morton White's article on "Original Sin, Natural Law and Politics," in *The Partisan Review*, Spring, 1956.

Equality is one of the oldest and deepest elements in liberal thought, and is neither more nor less "natural" or "rational" than any other constituent in them. Like all human ends it cannot itself be defended or justified, for it is itself that which justifies other acts—means taken towards its realisation. Many policies and views of life, themselves not particularly wedded to the ideal of equality, have been surreptitiously smuggled in under its cover, sometimes, as Mr. Wollheim suggests, with a certain measure of disingenuousness or hypocrisy. To isolate the pure ore of egalitarianism proper from those alloys which the admixture of other attitudes and ideals has at various times generated, is a task for the historian of ideas and lies outside the purpose of this paper.

SPECTRUM 🏛 PAPERBACKS

*Other SPECTRUM Books . . . quality paperbacks that
meet the highest standards of scholarship and integrity.*

About the Contributors

Henry Sidgwick *(1838-1900) is the author of* THE METHODS OF ETHICS, *a major philosophical work.* J. D. Mabbott *is a Fellow of St. John's College, Oxford University.* Jonathan Harrison *is a Lecturer in Moral Philosophy in the University of Edinburgh.* John Rawls *is a Professor of Philosophy, Massachusetts Institute of Technology.* Richard Wollheim *is a Lecturer in Philosophy in the University of London.* Sir Isaiah Berlin *is the Chichele Professor of Social and Political Theory, Oxford University.*